The Scouting Game

Chris Robinson

The Scouting Game

**An Insider's Guide
to Talent Spotting
Football's Next Stars**

First published by Pitch Publishing, 2025

Pitch Publishing
9 Donnington Park,
85 Birdham Road,
Chichester, West Sussex,
PO20 7AJ
www.pitchpublishing.co.uk
info@pitchpublishing.co.uk

A CIP catalogue record is available for this book
from the British Library.

ISBN 978 1 80150 924 4

Printed and bound on FSC® certified paper in line with
our continuing commitment to ethical business practices,
sustainability and the environment.

Typesetting and origination by Pitch Publishing

Printed and bound in India by Replika Press Pvt. Ltd.

Contents

Chapter One

It Starts and Ends with Players

99 per cent of scouting is saying no

THE SCOUTING game is a game of persistence and, in a sense, a numbers game. You have to accept you will be going to watch a lot of players and for the most part very few of them will be the players that you want or can realistically get. You need to have that patience and persistence. You need to get the perspective right otherwise you will run out of patience. Even when you have brought a player in for whatever is the next step, then you have to accept it will probably not be your decision as to whether they get signed or not. Your job is to watch them, identify and assess them and communicate that to the club. The rest is usually up to other people. That is the reality of scouting, and unless you come to terms with it then you will suffer.

One of my favourite parts of the scouting season is the period from around mid-August to October when there are the early rounds of the FA Youth Cup. This is where your local non-league teams will be putting up their best u18s (under-18s) to compete and hopefully find a way through to the later rounds when the big academies join in. You usually get to see a lot of good players in competitive games that they want to win.

For the great majority of games that I go to watch, I am on my own. I prefer this because I really concentrate on the game and I am not there to chat. Over the years I have come to know a lot of other scouts and it is great to catch up with them; however, when it comes to the game itself, I will often wander off a little and find a bit of space for myself and focus on what is in front of me.

So, on this occasion, it was indeed unusual that I had someone with me, and it was my wife, which was even more unusual! She loves sports, was a national-level gymnast and now runs a gymnastics business, so is very tuned into games and competition. I have also found that she is a good judge of which players move well, which is a key part of identification where players are concerned. Having said that, it is not usual by any means that she comes with me to games. This evening, though, she just felt like coming along, so I had company. I think she wanted to watch me work too, wondering perhaps what I get up to at all these games I go off to.

This was a lovely August evening, and the game was local to us, at Billingshurst in West Sussex. I am sure those facts helped her decision to tag along. We went for a nice meal at an Italian restaurant nearby before the game. This again was quite unusual. As a scout you get used to eating where and when you can. Too often it is a greasy underdone burger from a hut at the scruffy ground you are attending. Scouts will often recommend which grounds do good food or where there is a handy café near a ground. It is all part of the scouting culture. After the meal, we then went to Billingshurst FC's quite modern set-up with its little stands, which on this occasion had quite a few people there, as is often the case for the FA Youth Cup games. Family and friends may be drawn out to watch an FA Youth Cup game, particularly if it is a pleasant summer's evening like it was for this one. A night at Billingshurst watching u18 football! Who says I don't give a girl a good time?

Right from the warm-up Julie spotted the No. 10 of the opposing team and said how he looked quite sharp in his movement and quite agile. I like to be there to watch the warm-ups. You can get a feel for who is ready to work hard and who is maybe going through the motions. You can begin to get a picture of the social dynamics in a team. Who is lost in their own world or who is encouraging team-mates? When we are scouting we are searching for clues about players. Some may turn out to be relevant and others may be misleading red herrings.

As the game progressed, the opposition – Chipstead – were clearly the better team but it was a good competitive game for all that. Chipstead played a 4-3-3 and the No.10 played on the left side of the front three. He was quite slightly built but wiry, had very good left-foot touch and showed some considerable skill with the ball, being able to beat players quite easily. He was quite nippy too, and showed the good physical movement Julie had noted. I had got a team sheet by asking the club officials beforehand, so as I looked at his name I was sure there was something familiar about him. I sent a couple of WhatsApp messages and got it confirmed that he used to be with the club that I was working for, although he had left at the end of his u14 season. He had gone on to another pro academy but had obviously drifted out of that given he was here in front of me playing for a non-league u18 team. His team won 9-1 and he scored four goals. There were two guys who sat behind us who were scouts of some description and they were raving about him. Overall, I thought he had played well, and I also liked the left centre-back on his team, who I also recognised as having previously been in a Cat 3 academy for some years.

As we were driving home Julie was asking what I was going to do about this lad who had scored the goals. I said that he had had a good game, but he was playing poor opposition (with all due respect to Billingshurst) who were outclassed on the day. He was good on the ball, with a good left-foot touch, and a leftie is always interesting, but he did not work hard enough for me off the ball and only came alive when the ball was near him. He did not make much movement off the ball to create space, and was predictable. For these reasons I did not think he was going to be up to our standard, so while he played well, scoring four goals and was probably man of the match, he was not for me.

I did arrange to have him watched by a colleague in the next round of the FA Youth Cup, just to check up. On so many occasions I have either been very enthusiastic or dismissive about a player on just one showing and have learned that it can be misleading, so if there is the opportunity then it is worth getting that player cross-checked. Scouting is a team game. The conclusion came back from my colleague that he agreed with me. The player had talent and ability but lacked application and game understanding. So we passed on him.

However, I did like the left centre-back, although he was right-footed and would have been more interesting if he had been left-footed. But he read the game well, had a good profile physically and talked very well. He used the ball effectively and above all as a centre-back he could win the ball and defend. My colleague who watched the next round was also positive about him. I ended up inviting this centre-back into a series of showcase games we had for that age group, and although we did not take him in the end, he did go on to receive offers from other pro clubs. He was not the player that for most people would be the most attractive in the original game I watched and he probably would not get the headlines like the No.10 who scored the four goals. However, he was in a position that we were more interested in and was more of a priority for us. He displayed other elements in his game that showed longer-term promise. Crucially, I knew the standard and requirements that my club had.

So I said no to a player who had been the 'star' performer on the night but still had him checked out further. I said yes to another player who then did come to us, as I said, but again in the end we said no. There is a lot of saying no in scouting. The trick is knowing why it is a 'no' and when it is a 'yes'.

Follow this link to a video of me talking about that evening in Billingshurst:

Chapter Two

'Who Are You?'

IT STARTS and finishes with players. Scouting does and so does this book. Scouting is all about finding the right players. You must know what you are looking for.

Many years ago, I visited Nigeria. While there, I wanted to get one of those carved wooden elephants you see everywhere in Africa being sold on street corners. A local guy I knew said he would take me to where they make the best ones, and I could buy direct from there. So, he took me into the dusty, hot backstreets of Lagos, an area called Mushin, as I recall, where the people are mostly Yoruba. We came to an open workshop, which was basically just a tarpaulin shading some crude work benches, and he took me to one of the craftsmen – a wiry guy with long fingers and greying hair. I watched him work a while, then said to this guy, 'It's amazing, you take a block of wood and create an elephant from it.' I was in awe of his craftsmanship.

'It's easy,' shrugged the guy, 'you just knock off the bits that don't look like an elephant.'

We laughed. I bought the elephant (I still have it 40-plus years later). It was a good line and I have thought about it a lot over the years. I realised that he was, of course, right, but to say you just knocked off the bits that do not look like an elephant, then you really had to know what an elephant looked like. I mean, really know. Then it was easy.

I always say I can tell you the best and worst player in any football game within five minutes. I think any experienced scout can. It is all the buggers in between that are the challenge! It is also an issue to try to guess what the player in front of you would be like with better players around him and better coaching and conditioning, or playing in a different league or system, let alone guessing what shape, size and mentality they will have in five years' time if they are still children.

I always laugh when I read someone say, 'Oh, yes, I saw him play at seven and knew he would play for England.' Well, I always think, you need to come and do my job then, because I cannot tell that far ahead. If they are ten years old, I think a reasonable question to ask is: will they be in our top five if they came into our group now? Would they start if we were playing Manchester City next week in a Premier League tournament final? Will they be in our starting XI at u12? I think these are reasonable questions. But do not ask me whether they will play for the club's first team when they are 20. My answer would be 'I have no idea'.

But in scouting, as in life generally, I have definitely found it helps if you know what your elephant looks like. We will come to that.

So, I must say, the starting point when you begin your journey as a scout is to make sure you really know your own players. You must know what you are recruiting to. I know this sounds an obvious thing, but so often I see scouts, who are very keen to get started, just desperate to get out to games on the parks and 'find a player'. However, equally often when speaking to scouts about their own teams, they say, 'I don't get the chance to see them much actually.' This is so common and so crazy. How can you possibly judge whether the player you are watching is better than those you have if you do not know them?

I know it is tough if you work for an academy across various ages – there are a lot of players to watch in your own club. A lot of the better-resourced and better-organised clubs will make sure their scouts have access – via Hudl or whatever platform – to regular videos of their own age groups in games so that there is no excuse not to know the standard. There is an old military saying that 'time spent on reconnaissance is never wasted', and I would say it applies here. Know the elephants you already have, as a start.

But why am I writing a book on scouting? Firstly, I do not think many people understand what scouting involves. Every player that you watch on TV each week or pay good money to go along to watch, has been scouted at some point. It is a vital step in the pathway to being a top player. Someone must see you somewhere and say 'yes'. However, scouting remains an undervalued and misunderstood part of the game. Scouts are not recognised and respected as much as they should be. They are often forgotten along the way. They are usually poorly paid, if paid at all, and ignored. I want to try to put that right in some way and put scouts on the map.

Secondly, there are not many books at all on this subject. Yet people seem fascinated by how scouting works. So many times when people hear what I do for a living, they ask, 'What do you look for?' People also say, 'What a great job you have – how do you get into scouting?' Then there are many parents out there who are desperate for their kids to become professional footballers. They want to know what we in the professional game are looking for and they have a lot of practical questions, like 'what happens on a trial?' These may be questions about subjects that those in the game take for granted. But parents may well not know the ins and outs of academies, for example, if they are new to the scene, or how a contract works. So, from all sorts of angles – people who would like to be scouts, football fans generally interested in the inner workings of the game we love and parents trying to understand how the pathways into the game work – there seems to be a lot of people interested in the subject and little real information out there.

But why do I think I should be the one writing it? I do not suggest I know it all and, as in all sports, I am constantly learning. There are many experienced scouts out there; however, there are not many people who have had the range of experience I have had across scouting – from grassroots, from the pre-academy ages of six and seven, right up through academy scouting and senior scouting including first team, opposition, video and international work. I have worked for various clubs, including managing clubs such as Cheltenham Town FC, and running a development centre for Portsmouth FC for seven- and eight-year-old players, which meant coaching and scouting there. Then I had over 11 years at Chelsea FC in a senior position in the recruitment team at the academy. I have been around the block where scouting is concerned.

I do not think many people in the game would disagree that Chelsea have one of the foremost academies in the world. I learned so much from so many top people in my 11 years there. For the last seven years, I was 'Head of Integration Scouting' there and have also been involved in managing and training scouts.

I want this to be a comprehensive guide to all the major facets of scouting in the modern football world (albeit from a UK perspective). We will look at how players are assessed – what the main criteria are that are used to judge a player. We will look at what, in my view, are the key performance indicators for each position and we will also look at what we know now about the key elements in performance. We will consider what makes a difference in a game and what we as scouts should look for.

Scouting is the last part of football to be professionalised. For many years it was the preserve of middle-aged white men who made back-of-a-fag-packet reports. But it is changing. It became obvious that assessing a player was one thing but communicating that assessment was something else.

This takes us into the realms of report writing, internet systems, big data and comparing players – the brave new world that scouting finds itself in. We will look at how you communicate your views on players and what information is around to help you.

You still see vestiges of the old regime about. A couple of years ago I went to Crawley Town to watch a Brighton u23 game against Wolves. It was a cold wintry night and not much of a crowd was there at all. I went to the main entrance, found the reception and got my ticket. I went through into a lounge where the usual suspects were gathered, hunched over stewed cups of tea, grabbing the few bland biscuits left out and gossiping in small furtive bunches.

I think there were about 15 scouts there for that game. They were nearly all middle-aged or elderly white men (like me). When we were all sat down at the game, I noticed a few things. Firstly, a lot of them were more involved in gossiping than watching the game. Secondly, only one other scout – a younger guy – and I were taking notes of the game. Thirdly, half of them left ten minutes from the end.

I go to a game to watch the play. That is my job. I do have a lot of friends who are scouts and I enjoy meeting up with them at games, having some chat and exchanging information, and, of course, networks are important. But once it kicks off, my job is to watch the bloody game!

Also, maybe those guys had much better memories than me, but I need to make notes to remember details and to enable me to report properly on those players. Maybe most of those guys were still the old-fashioned type of scout whose idea of reporting back was a phone call on the way home to their head of recruitment.

'Yeah? Hello mate. Yes, he played. He was okay, quite quick but I didn't fancy him. Not for us. No, he was injured, didn't play. They lost two-nil. Yeah, crap game.'

What? Why wasn't he for us? What did he do well? What position did he play? Who was he up against? What were his weaknesses? How does he compare with what we have? Is that it?

Lastly, I can possibly understand that if you are at a game with a big crowd and it is really difficult to get away, you may leave a couple of minutes early to beat the hordes. However, at that game, there were just a handful of people there anyway. What if they had thrown on a young kid for his debut off the bench in the last ten minutes and he took the game by storm?

We do see elements of poor practice, old-fashioned attitudes and sheer laziness from fellow scouts along the way. We are undervalued, as I have said, and I will explain why I think that. However, some of us do not help the cause. We all have our biases and we will look at the thorny problems this throws up too.

Scouting is changing and has changed. Even in grassroots scouting many clubs now look for feedback reports from scouts after games. At some academies they now have apps for scouts' phones that they can fill out after every game. It takes about a minute, but records basic facts, the date and any standout players. Data and feedback are gathered and your views as scout, your opinions, can be properly assessed.

Many of the old dinosaurs struggle with the new tech, of course. When I decided I was going to focus more on scouting than coaching and managing, some years ago, I did an online course via the League Managers Association on 'using data in football'. This course was run by Robin Russell, formerly of the FA, and the Sports Path people, and it was excellent. I was determined I would not get lost behind all the generations of sports science graduates coming out of our universities now every year. I knew I had the experience in the game and believed I had the 'eye' for scouting, but I knew I had to get to grips with managing information and data. I will talk later about the data world too.

I want to cover scouting senior players as well as kids and opposition scouting. When someone tells me they would like to be a scout I usually ask, 'What sort of scout? Grassroots? Academy? Senior? Opposition? Video?' I want to cover all these bases in the book.

I will talk about agents too, much maligned, and sometimes rightly so, but a significant resource for scouts, and certainly a part of our game now across almost all ages. Equally, I would expect that some of the people reading this book might be agents or prospective agents too. There are a lot of people working in talent identification for the agencies, and the issues and settings in identifying talent are much the same for them as they are for scouts, of course.

I will set out some of the pathways into scouting, how you can become a scout and some of the training available. I will also paint you a picture of what the realities of being a scout and scouting are like, the pros and cons.

I must stress now that all I am setting out here is my opinion – not the views of the clubs I have worked for or anyone else. I am not suggesting all this is entirely original either. I have had the advantage of working alongside some of the very best scouts in the modern game and, of course, I have taken on board what I have seen and adapted their practices. They will probably appear in the book, too. It is based on my experience, and in a sense the expertise of many I have worked alongside.

I should add, too, that throughout I have referred to the players as masculine – I invariably say what 'he' can do and so on. This is for two reasons. Firstly, I need to find some terms that allow the sentences to roll on, and saying 'he/she' or 'they' all the time does not always allow my words to flow. Secondly, virtually all of my experience has been in scouting in the boys' and men's game, so it is natural for me to reflect on that experience. I do not mean to be sexist and am not denigrating the emerging women's game at all, and I will look at some of the specific issues of the girls' and women's game in the book.

Football is our passion, of course, and the 'beautiful game' is our inspiration. It is that passion and love that keeps us going out in all weathers to all sorts of places. However, football is a small world – if you are in professional football as a player, scout, coach, manager or whatever, then even if we do not know each other we will have people that we both know, for sure. Just one step removed from everyone.

But it is also a very insecure and at times cruel world. It is great when you tell a young kid and their parents that you would like the lad to come in for a trial. It is usually such an exciting thing for them. Telling them they are going to be signed is even better! However, I have had to do the 'thanks but no thanks' speech on many more occasions and it is tough. In the professional game, we are involved in elite sport. It is about selection and filtering to find the best. It is not 'sport for all'. Decisions must be made, and they can make or break someone's dreams – often a whole family's dreams. I will look at how these key decisions are made and how they are conveyed.

If you do work at the top of the game, then I must say there is huge expectation and pressure. I work about 60 hours a week – plus the phone calls and WhatsApp messages 24 hours a day, and work about 11 months of the year. If we are not successful, then people lose jobs. Sometimes jobs are lost even when we are winning. It can be an arbitrary and unfair arena, too.

If you want to come into this crazy world or get a child into it, then you need to know the reality. That is what I am aiming to show you in this book.

For all that, I still get a buzz going to a game to scout. You never quite know what you are going to find. The surge of adrenaline when you see a player that excites you is terrific. It remains a fascinating and challenging line of work to be in, with always something more to learn. There is always another game, always another player. Always another elephant.

See my video introduction to the book here:

Chapter Three

What Are We Looking For?

THE MOST common question I am asked when people find out I am a scout is: 'What do you look for in a player?' In this chapter, I want to try to answer that question.

I should first talk about *performance* and *potential*. When we go to watch a player, we are firstly assessing their performance on that day, in the game in front of us. Regardless of the opposition or the level or the pitch (although noting all those things), we are assessing how they played. That is *performance*. However, often as a scout we are trying to consider what that player might become. Maybe it is a question of what they might become in a different team, a different system, with different players around them or with a different coach, possibly in a different league at a different level. If they are a young player we usually try also to consider how they might develop. What shape and size might they be when they are 20 years old? This can be notoriously difficult to estimate. We are in the realm of educated guesses. But here we are looking at *potential*.

There are more scientific tests possible – and I will mention them later – but when you are judging a player from the sidelines you must make some rough and ready assessments. In terms of guessing at the future height of a young player, the old standby, of course, is to see how tall their parents are. This may be a useful guide – it is an old trope that sons always outgrow their mothers, for example. I have not heard the same old saying applied to daughters though! However, you might not know initially who their parents are, so that may not be a practical guess you can make at that stage. You will develop your own rough and ready initial assessments. Generally, for example, I have found that if a lad's legs are longer than his torso then he has more growing to do. You will make your own judgements. Whether it is guessing at future physical growth or the development of footballing ability or emotional maturity, we are looking into a crystal ball, and that is all about *potential*.

I mention the two things *performance* and *potential* here now and will refer later to them when looking at reporting to clarify their difference, because they are often mixed up in assessments and conversations in the scouting world.

Player Assessment Criteria

We need to agree on how we are going to assess the player in front of us.

Football is based on control, pass and move, and variations and developments of these three pillars. An experienced scout I know, once told me, 'What matters most is their first touch and their last.' I can see their point and it has stuck with me: can they control it, can they pass, and then who is it to? It is a great starting point.

It is all about control and passing in possession. Shooting is essentially a development of passing, of striking the ball. Also, we need to win the ball, so we must add competing too. Now, probably every club has a slightly different set of criteria to assess players and then rate them. It is also true that assessing a six-year-old is going to be different to assessing a prospective first-team adult player. However, I think it is generally true that most assessment systems reflect the 'four-corner' type of model that the FA and many others use, in one way or another. This is referred to a lot in coaching and talent ID courses. So that is a good place to start and a good guide to grouping the criteria for identifying football talent.

The four-corner model commonly follows this sort of pattern:

TECHNICAL	PSYCHOLOGICAL
PHYSICAL	SOCIAL

For scouting though, I think we can adjust this a little where player assessment is concerned:

TECHNICAL	PSYCHOLOGICAL
PHYSICAL	TACTICAL

Let's look at what questions we might be asking to assess a player in each of these categories:

Technical

Can they control the ball? This is the starting point – but will then take us into:

- Can they control it at any pace or height?
- With either foot?
- Can they use their body to control it?
- Do they use their first touch to direct the ball – maybe away from an opponent or in a first-time pass?

- Can they control the ball under pressure?
- John Terry had a very good first touch. He could knock the ball off to his left-back with one touch off either foot, use his chest or head it there. But he could also do it when he had Andy Carroll in his ribs. Completing the task is a *technique*. Doing it under pressure is a *skill*. If you watch the warm-ups, as I like to do, you can see players who seem to have ability. They display *techniques*, usually their favourite ones in controlling or juggling the ball or whatever – but maybe we will not get to see their skills until the pressure of the game. It is important for a scout to recognise the difference. We have all come across players who look good in training when there is often less pressure and yet struggled in games when the going got tough.

Can they pass the ball?

- Can they pass it with either foot?
- Can they strike the ball cleanly?
- Can they pass it accurately over 5m and over 40m?
- Can they pass the ball with a lofted chip over an opponent?
- Can they use swerve or spin to pass the ball around an opponent?

- Can they shoot? This is an extension of passing, of course.
- Can they pass accurately under pressure?
- Can they pass well using one touch?

Can they win the ball?

- Can they tackle and win the ball, staying on their feet?
- Can they jockey and press an opponent using their body position?

Every player, whatever position, must contribute to defending as well as attacking. Basically, when we have the ball as a team, we are attacking – wherever the ball is. When they have the ball, we are defending – again, wherever the ball is. When we are watching defenders, we really need to see them under pressure when their one-on-one defending becomes vital. If a team is winning easily and dominating play, then it may be the case that their defenders are having an easy time and are rarely under pressure. This can be particularly true when it comes to two centre-backs playing against a single striker. The centre-back who tends to sit off can have an easy ride in many ways. We can only judge what is in front of us. So, we would be looking for communication, pass choice, covering positions, response to transitions in the play and so on. We are, as ever, searching for clues. In this situation it may be vital that we watch the defender again, hopefully in a more challenging game.

We will be wary of a defender who dives in – sometimes a player will seek to compensate for their lack of pace or must make up for their poor positioning by diving into a sliding tackle. This can look impressive at times but should always raise the question as to whether it was necessary and why it was necessary.

All players need to contribute to winning the ball back. In the modern game the immediate counter-press where a coach expects his team to immediately switch into active defensive mode and chase the ball down when they lose it highlights the need for everyone to be able to contribute. Again we must note that this type of pressing is to some extent age-specific in that we may not expect u9s to do this, but certainly would be looking for u14s to be doing it. I would argue, though, that the basic desire to win the ball back is important at all ages.

Can they head the ball?

- Can they direct a header to where they want the ball to go?
- Can they win and head a ball under pressure?

Okay, this is a controversial area now and I know there is a lot of discussion about banning heading. I was doing a video assessment of a u10 player in the USA recently and was momentarily confused when an indirect free kick was given against a player just because he headed the ball. Then I remembered it is now the norm in parts of the USA for heading to be taken out of the game at an early age. I guess there is a little sidenote here about being aware of differing rules and customs in different countries when it comes to international scouting. This is not the place to go through the arguments for and against heading as such.

It is still part of the game for most ages in most countries – certainly in the UK – so it needs assessing. It is also a dying art in many ways. Few players can demonstrate good heading technique. Some are reluctant to head the ball and will avoid it if at all possible. So many times, we see an attacking player in front of goal head the ball up. The default should be to head the ball down in that situation, but young players are rarely taught how to head the ball properly and this exacerbates the injury chances too. The rule of thumb is that if we do not have a team-mate around to direct the ball to – which will be first choice – then a defensive header is away and up and an attacking header is at the goal and down. It could perhaps be argued that it will not be necessary to legislate against heading in the UK game because it is dying out anyway!

Can they finish?

- Do they score goals?
- Can they stay composed enough to direct shots and headers at goal?
- Are they able to finish under pressure?
- Can they make a range of finishes – tap-ins, longer shots, goals from crosses, one-on-ones?

The best finisher I ever saw was Jimmy Greaves, my first hero, who talked about 'passing the ball into the net', and this is the sign of a composed finisher. On the other hand, I worked for a few years for Sir Bobby Charlton, and he was famous for being able to blast a ball into the net, with either foot, incidentally, from a distance. He had been encouraged by Jimmy Murphy, his coach at Manchester United, to 'keep shooting, even if they hit the corner flag' when a young player, and he had great technique. A top striker such as Harry Kane scores all sorts of goals. You might ask whether this is relevant for a defender. Well, in the modern game everyone is expected to chip in with some goals and it is good to know whether a centre-back, for example, can finish well too.

Once again, we see players who can finish when they are in space and time, and that is fine, but we also want to see whether they can get their shot away when under pressure. It also brings to mind great strikers such as Luca Vialli and Hernán Crespo, because when I saw them live for the first time I noticed in both cases that they tended to shoot 'early' rather than take too many touches that moved them away from the goal. They were shooting when they had most of the goal to aim at. In addition, other top strikers such as Jimmy Floyd Hasselbaink and Ian Wright would seem to direct their shots almost towards the keeper's legs but invariably hard and on target. Their goals tally proves their point. So we look for what types of finishing a player can accomplish and what their habits are.

Physical

The modern game is very quick, and at all levels fitness and mobility are required even if to different degrees. Not every player needs to be over six feet tall, although some managers do prefer bigger players. When I was in Italy last summer, I read that Jose Mourinho had a lot of outfield players over 190cm (6ft 3in) in his squad.

However, height is not always a requirement. N'Golo Kanté is not tall, but he is very strong and very mobile. Whatever the position or type of player, the physical side of the game will be important. Pace is a key decider in assessing a player in many cases, and power and agility are essential to some degree. There clearly is a place for the smaller player – Messi, for example! But his wiriness and athleticism are major positives for him too.

Are they quick and agile?

- Are they quick over 3m and 30m?
- If there was a footrace of all the players, where would they finish?
- Are they agile?
- Can they turn quickly?
- Are they light on their feet?

Pace is so important in the modern game, which is quick at the top levels. It is played by extremely fit and mobile players. It is one of the attributes that translates up the levels. By this, I mean that if a player has real pace, then this will apply as they go higher and will still be an asset. When you are a scout, though, when watching a lower-level game, it can be quite difficult to identify how quick a player might be. They can seem quick in the context of that particular game at that level, but will they still seem so if they play higher? This can be difficult to judge and is one of the reasons that often the first thing a club will do with a player coming in on trial is to measure their pace in order to compare it against the rest of the squad's testing results. Within a game you are looking for those instances when there is a 'footrace'. These might be few and far between, maybe when there is a ball over the top and a defender races an attacker to get there. I have often come away from a game saying, 'I like the player; he has this or that, but I am not sure how quick he is.' The only way to know, short of getting any physical testing data on the player, is to watch them again and look for those key moments where pace is needed.

It is a debatable question as to how much better training and conditioning can improve a player's absolute pace. Their running technique can be worked on, and their agility and movement skills can be improved. Their reading of the game can be improved – 'the first five metres are in your head' is a well-known saying among scouts, but I am not sure how much absolute pace can be improved. My good friend Ruben Tabares – the best strength and conditioning coach in my opinion – assures me that virtually everyone's pace can be improved. He knows better than me in this field too.

Are they strong?

- Can they hold off opponents?
- Can they protect the ball under pressure?
- Do they use their body well?
- Do they have good spring?

As mentioned, you do not need to be six feet-plus to play football. We know that. You do need to be strong though, whatever shape or size. Again, strength can be improved but it would help if a player was robust enough to show that they can compete, they can challenge.

Once again, though, when it comes to young players, we will be considering that they have a lot of growing to do and trying to consider where they might be in terms of their physical development. In this sense, it is about making conscious judgements as a scout, or perhaps educated guesses.

Are they fit?

- Is their stamina good?
- Do they get around well and cover ground?
- Are they as mobile in the last five minutes as the first?
- Can they keep working until the end?

You might say that they will get fitter if we sign them. Yes, we can expect that, hopefully. But in the context of the game we are watching we need to gauge a player's fitness. If we are from a higher level of football, then if we bring a player in they may struggle to show what they can do if they are struggling initially to keep up, and this can lead to them losing confidence and not showing their best. It can really help if the player can cope physically with whatever our level is to begin with. It is also a hint at their attitude and preparation. If a young player tells me they desperately want to be a professional footballer, then I do expect them to be really fit and will ask them what their fitness programme consists of. It does not have to be visiting a gym every day, but if they demonstrate an awareness of how they can be in the best possible shape given their situation, it would be encouraging.

Do they move well?

- Do they run with a fluid, easy motion?

There are examples of players with awkward running styles who are still, in fact, quick and can cope with the pace of the modern game. However, there are not many! As players go up the football pyramid the physical demands get tougher and those who move well will usually find it easier to adapt and improve. Another worry when a player does not move well is that they may be more prone to injuries as they grow. For young players aged six and seven, for example, this natural easy movement is a major plus; however, we know some very young players are still moving like toddlers at that stage and this will be an immediate but maybe not a long-term issue.

When it comes to assessing grassroots players, I must say that their agility and the capacity to move easily and fluently and be light on their feet are very common areas of concern. A player may be good technically but struggle to change direction or lack balance. This can be worked on, of course, but it is off-putting to scouts and something players with ambitions of the pro game could attend to themselves by getting some movement training. They could look at going to a gymnastics coach or athletic coach, for example.

Psychological

The mental side of the game is so important. At the elite level we are invariably looking at players who are good technically and physically. The aspect that picks out those who are really top and will go on to deliver on their potential is invariably character. I cannot stress this enough. When we watch a player in a game, we might not know that player well, or even at all. So, we are looking for clues as to their character. A winning mentality is so important. Football is tough, and you need people who really want to win. There will be a rocky road too, so you need players who can overcome setbacks.

We sometimes find that the young player who was the best player in their school, then the best in their grassroots club and who went on to an academy and sailed through as a star player suddenly hits a wall and struggles. They may not have developed resilience, the capacity to overcome setbacks. They may lack 'grit'. This wall may be the step up to senior football, for example, or serious injury or other setback. There will be setbacks along the path to and into a professional football career. I can guarantee you that. Players need to develop resilience, and identifying how they deal with problems and setbacks is a key part of scouting. This may not be easy, of course, if we do not know the player, but it is something that a scout must bear in mind.

Are they brave?

- Are they physically brave?
- Are they emotionally brave?

There are different types of bravery – notably physical and emotional. In the games we can look for physical bravery. How do they respond to physical challenges? Are they ready to put their body on the line at times with a block, a last-ditch tackle or a brave diving header? But there is also the emotional bravery required to make yourself available and want to get on the ball when things are going badly for your team or for you as an individual player. When it is tough do they go and hide? The brave player in this context will be the one still showing for the ball, still making the runs, still asking for the ball when his team is under the cosh.

Are they a winner?

- Are they persistent?
- What do they do when they lose the ball?
- Can they cope with setbacks?
- Can they control themselves?

Does it matter to them if their team wins or loses? I was once looking at a young player aged about nine and it was a cup final. I spoke to his dad and the lad after the game, which the lad's team had lost. The lad was in tears. His dad apologised for his crying. 'Not at all,' I said, 'it's good to know it matters to him.'

However, if the lad was 16 and burst into tears in the middle of a game I *would* begin to worry!

Do they concentrate?

- Do they keep a focus on the game?
- Do they get involved negatively with the ref or other officials?
- How do they interact with comments from the sidelines (e.g. parents)?

Sometimes a young player will automatically look to their parents whenever anything happens in the game. This can be understandable at a young age but will be a worry as the player grows up. They must be able to make their own decisions, and if they are receiving information or instruction it should be from their coach, not their parents. A player who gets tied up in a running battle with an opponent or, even worse, with the referee, could well be in danger of getting distracted and losing focus. This would be a worry. Some players thrive on the conflict – Diego Costa comes to mind – but, generally, we want players focused on the game.

It still amazes me how many players at the top level get needlessly booked for arguing with the referee or by silly actions such as kicking a ball away. This is just ill-discipline. We see top coaches doing it too. None of this is good for their own teams, nor does it set a good example for the young players watching.

Do they work hard?

- What do they do when they lose the ball?
- What do they do immediately after they have passed the ball?
- Do they run as fast working back as going forward?
- How does their work rate compare in the last 15 minutes to the first 15 minutes?

Whatever the state of the game or the form a player is in, there is no excuse not to work hard. So many times I have come away from games feeling that the player I have watched showed ability on or near the ball but 'switched off' when the ball was not near. Their game awareness was poor. They perhaps passed and then stood back and admired the effect rather than moving up to support, for example. All these examples would worry me as a scout.

Football is a team game. One way or another, players must combine, and they must cope with a team context. We would always make allowances for the individual character of a player. We do not want everyone to be the same or react the same. But I do recall reading about how the All Blacks rugby team reinvented themselves and developed their incredible team spirit, and their number-one rule was apparently 'no arseholes'! A player who does not work hard enough is going to be an issue somewhere down the line, whatever their talent level.

How do they interact with team-mates?

- Are they positive with team-mates?
- Do they encourage others?
- Are they a 'moaner'?
- How do they react to the coaches' instructions?

Searching for clues about the psychological make-up of a player and how they interact with their team-mates is an interesting area. Even making allowances for individual differences, if a player is constantly moaning at team-mates, reacting negatively and never encouraging them, then it stands to reason that they are going to be a difficult player to play with. Again, with many of these things, they are not necessarily a final negative, but they would be a cause for concern and something that I, as a scout, would make a note of and want to enquire further into when I am beginning to learn more about the player. And if a player was positive, gave good information to their team-mates and was encouraging them and driving them on in a positive way, then this would be a real plus point in my report. If you can hear what the player is saying to their team-mates, then you might also be able to get an understanding of the extent of the game awareness of the player in question.

To be able to take on instruction from a coach is also important. If we are looking at recruiting a player aged 14, let's say from grassroots football into an academy, then we know they will have a lot to learn. It is going to be important that they can take on coaching instructions, learn from them and put them into action. I might note here that a very interesting exercise is when we are looking at a player in a trial or in a development centre assessing players; you get the coach to play that player out of their normal position and give them simple instructions. These instructions might be what to do when their team is in possession and what to do when they are out of possession, and they will be very simple. So, for example, you might say to a striker that you want him to play at full-back. You might say, 'When we have the ball I want you to get wide and push up and when they have the ball I want you to tuck in as a back four and look to pick up a man should there be one near to you.' The point is to put them just out of their comfort zone but also to see if they can follow simple coaching instructions. If you have players in for a single trial game it might not work doing this, but if you have a little more time it is an interesting idea. If within a normal game context we can see a coach giving our player some instructions, then it is always interesting to be able to follow up and see whether they put those instructions into action.

Do they communicate?

- Do they shout for the ball?
- Do they communicate with their team-mates?

Effective communication with your team-mates is a key part of the modern game. However, to get young players (and particularly teenage boys) to even speak on a pitch at times can be challenging. I think this may be because there is a tendency nowadays for someone not to want to be seen as telling someone else what to do. This is just not adequate on a football pitch, of course. It is not a question of telling your team-mate what to do but it is an important element of helping your team-mate by giving them information and by encouraging them to do the right thing.

We will certainly be aware of this in relation to goalkeepers. However, with goalkeepers, as with all players, it is not just a matter of them talking or shouting but it is a question of them giving the *right* information at the *right* time. I have often seen goalkeepers who are very chatty when play has gone down the other end and they are pushing up into a good starting position and encouraging their team-mates from there, but then when the pressure is on and they really need to communicate important information, the requirement seems to slip their mind.

Football is a team game and part of working as a team is to communicate with each other. If a player does not have this attribute in their locker, then it is a question of whether you think they are going to be able to acquire it. They will need it.

Tactical

At younger ages we will inevitably focus more on the technical and physical aspects of performance. However, by the time a player gets to 12 or 13 years of age we would want to see them developing an understanding of the game and showing key awareness attributes that we can group together as 'Tactical'. Certainly, by the time they are 16 years of age, we need players to be able to take on board tactical information and to 'see' the game better. What we don't always know when we are watching a game, is the tactical instructions a player has already been given by his coach. However, in the absence of that info – and incidentally, it is good to be within earshot of the dugout if you can, so you can hear what tactical instructions players are being given – all we can go off is the principles of good play, as we understand them, and judge a player against those.

Are they aware of other players?

- Do they scan around, checking their shoulders?
- Can they play first-time passes to players around them?
- Do they track runners?
- Do they spot danger?
- Do they spot opportunity?

We will want players to be able to play quickly at a good tempo, and one of the ways that the really good players can do this is that they already know what is around them when they receive the ball. This is not due to some inbuilt radar or dark art, but it is a question of them scanning or checking their shoulders. If you watch a top midfield player, they are doing this all the time. This is a learned behaviour, so it can be added and can become a habit. However, if a player does not have this by their mid-teens, it is just another thing that you will have to consider whether they can take on board if they step up in standard. If they know where the nearest opponent is, their first touch can take them away from that opponent and it makes the game so much easier. Jorginho of Arsenal is not the quickest midfielder, but his touch and awareness of other players are so good that he can operate in tight spaces and move the ball well. His first touch will invariably take the ball away from his nearest opponent, or he is so adept at passing that one touch is enough anyway. Again, it is often the simple things that a player can do, such as simple one-touch passes, taking the ball out of pressure, that indicate their understanding of the game.

When you watch some defenders, you get the feeling that they are not aware of players getting in behind them, and this is a big red flag. Similarly, if you are watching a midfielder and they do not track runners when they need to and they do not seem to be aware of where the opposition is going or of the need to pass on opponents to team-mates, then as they get older this will be a matter of concern. A key attribute of a good defender is to be able to spot danger. By this I mean they can make an instant decision on what the priority is in terms of where they go. If an opposition player is breaking through, then at some point that defender will have to decide whether they are going to try to confront them and block them or whether they hold off, perhaps marking another opponent. We would be looking for those defenders who understand where the greatest point of danger is and move accordingly.

At the other end of the pitch, when going forward, it is again a question of whether a player's decision-making reflects a real understanding of the game. Do they know when to go on and take a shot themselves or when to pass? All these decision-making issues are more and more important as a player gets older. We can see players who are playing at a good level and have good fitness and a good physical profile, and even good basic skill, but they struggle to make an impact in a game because their decisions are not consistently good enough.

Do they make good decisions?

- Do they pick the right pass?
- At the right time?
- Do they know when to go forward and when to go back?
- Do they know when to tackle and when to drop off?

- Do they know when to shoot
  and when not to?
- Do they switch play at the right time?
- Do they play forward when they can?

When I have been assessing players coming from grassroots into an academy set-up, it is most often game awareness where they fall short. If they have not had the benefit of growing up in a good academy system with good coaching or developed that themselves, it is their decision-making that they may struggle with. Players can get away with lots of touches or selfishness on the ball when playing at a lower standard. When stepping up they may find it difficult to adjust if their decisions are not usually in as intense settings. Some players adjust quickly, while others struggle. As a scout it is difficult to know how they will fare in this regard when they need to improve.

A player's reaction to transitions is a key aspect to be considered. The many transitions in a game are when the ball changes hands: if your team wins the ball back, it is an attacking transition; if your team loses the ball, it is a defensive transition. Every player should have a clear picture in their heads of their two key tasks: what they should do when their team has the ball and what they should do when the other team has the ball. Consequently, arguably, every player should adjust their position on each transition. A player's reaction to transitions is therefore an illuminating and important aspect of performance for a scout to focus on.

Do they have good game intelligence?

- Do they adjust their play according to the state of the game?
- Do they help other players with tactical/positional info?
- Do they adjust their position when their team wins the ball?
- Do they adjust their position when their team loses the ball?

Game intelligence – reading the game, understanding when priorities in a game shift and adjusting your play accordingly – is a key skill set for the professional player. It can be learned and often comes through experience. As such it would not be something you would expect to see or particularly look for in players under the age of 12. However, beyond that you would want this more mature vision of the game to be influencing decisions and to be developing as they progress. Again, as a scout, the ideal would be to see players in different situations – winning, losing, struggling, coasting – but this is not always possible.

Do they have good movement?

- Do they make good runs or adjust their position to find space in possession?
- Do they vary their runs?
- Do they run offside a lot?
- Do they cover well to deny space to the opposition?
- Can they press well?

Very few players develop good movement without being coached in it. Very few grassroots players will have received good coaching, to be honest. So, it is often another of the facets of performance where you must make a judgement as to whether the player can learn. Even if we are looking to move a senior player up a couple of leagues, much the same applies – how will they respond to further coaching?

I must stress again that a lot of these criteria are age-related. At six years of age we would be more interested in whether the player has the basic technique sorted – can he control and pass – and whether he moves well, the physical literacy stuff. Gradually all the other factors and the various aspects of each factor come into our consideration until from around 16 onwards you are entitled to judge a player against every one of these criteria.

It is unfortunately rare to see a striker, for example, who moves away from a defender to make space they can then run into. Similarly, midfielders who know when they should drop off to make an easy angle for a pass and when to move ten metres higher up the pitch to hurt the opposition more from there are quite rare. We will see defenders marking from the wrong side or not opening their bodies up to help see the ball and the opponent they are marking. All these sorts of movement can be taught, as we have said, but are encouraging and welcome features in a player you are scouting.

If a player has been in the academy system for some years at a top level, we might expect much more than if they are a grassroots player 'off the parks', as we say. In those sorts of circumstances what we probably most want to know of a promising player is whether they are a good learner. If a player is coming into an academy system at age 13 or above, they will inevitably have a lot of catching up to do – in all four of these categories above – so they need to be someone who wants to learn and can learn.

At the senior level we might be recruiting for a particular type of player to play within a certain system. This will change what we are looking for, of course. If our head coach plays a high line of defence, then every defender is going to have to be quick. If we play out from the back, then we need defenders who are comfortable on the ball and so on.

The requirements of our elephants at any one time may change or be very specific. Again, we need to know what our elephant looks like at that moment we are scouting.

The Key Indicators of Performance

We have looked at how we assess an individual player. Now we need to delve a bit deeper into how we assess a team's performance and thus an individual's performance within a team game. We need to understand what the key indicators of team success in a game are to understand how our individual player is contributing to that success or not, as the case may be.

On one superficial level the key indicators are obvious – which team scores more goals? But, of course, if we start to delve a bit deeper we soon come up against other questions. What way of playing increases your chances of scoring more goals than the opposition? What way of playing increases your goal-scoring chances and limits theirs?

I learned early on in my coaching career that the answer to virtually every coaching question is 'it depends'. There are so many fascinating variables in football that it does mean nearly every question about ways of playing and the best systems and indicators needs a qualified answer.

Again, I might start with players. If you have Lionel Messi, you might play differently than if you have Cristiano Ronaldo up front. More than that, if you have a Messi or a Ronaldo you might well have a better chance of winning against a team that does not! However, we know it is not only about who has the best players – as significant as that undoubtedly is. How many times have we seen the 'better team' with the 'better players' get beat? When Chelsea won the UEFA Champions League in 2012, beating Bayern Munich in their own stadium, Bayern had 39 shots and Chelsea nine. Bayern had 20 corners to Chelsea's one (and scored from that, as I recall). Nevertheless, Chelsea won. (Sorry, I just had to use that example!)

As the modern game has evolved, we have seen various views come to the surface on what is the best way to increase your chances of success. When I was starting my coaching journey – I did my first coaching badge (the old 'FA Preliminary Award') in 1990 – through the 80s and early 90s the predominant view in this country about maximising the success of teams was that initially developed by Wing Commander Charles Reep in the 50s, when this accountant from an RAF background began to apply his understanding of numbers to football. He began to annotate, to analyse games. From all this developed the view that passing the ball around was not a key indicator of success. Winning the ball back in the opponent's third (essentially pressing) and getting the ball up into the key danger area quickly were the twin pillars of success. Hence, over time, the 'long ball game' was promoted as the most efficient way to win games. This was adopted by the English FA among others, when Charles Hughes was director of coaching for the FA from 1990, and his book *The Winning Formula* was the bible. If you did an FA coaching course in that era you were told you had to coach this way of playing. That was it.

Consequently, certain types of players became more valuable if your team was going to play that way. Full-backs that were adept at hitting long balls. Long-throw experts (Tony Pulis's Stoke, of course, brought this aspect to a fine art, if it can be called that, with Rory Delap's missile-launching). Hard-running, big, strong strikers. Workhorses in midfield. This is not the place or time to go into the whole history of different styles of play – this has been done very well elsewhere.[1] The point here is that the prevailing view of what is the best way to be successful at the game influences the sort of players you are looking for.

Later, the wonderful player and coach Johan Cruyff famously said, 'Without the ball, you can't win ... If we have the ball, they can't score.' So, we saw Barcelona spearhead a delightful way of playing based on passing and keeping possession. This was, of course, subsequently adopted by many coaches around the world, including Arsène Wenger at Arsenal. Again, this determined the type of player who was in demand from those coaches wanting to play a certain way. For example, a Cesc Fàbregas would not have been as successful in a long-ball team. However, he was ideally suited to the passing and possession game of Barcelona and Arsenal.

So, for many years possession stats were seen as the key. The idea was that the more you kept the ball, the better your chances of winning. This meant goalkeepers needed to be able to play out from the back, defenders needed to be comfortable on the ball to play round the opposition ('to beat the press') and

---

1   I would recommend *Inverting the Pyramid: The History of Soccer Tactics* by Jonathan Wilson (2013) and *The Numbers Game* by Chris Anderson and David Sally (2013).

so on. But that mantra of possession and passing did not always work out. When Brazil played Germany in the 2014 World Cup semi-finals, possession was quite even (Brazil 47 per cent, Germany 53 per cent). Brazil had more shots overall (18:14), more blocked shots (5:2) and more corners (7:5). Yet Brazil lost 7-1.[2] There was clearly more to winning a game than having more of the ball, even more than having a lot of the ball in the opponents' half.

We also saw how the passing football of Arsenal under Wenger ran into the sand as teams worked them out, sitting back, absorbing pressure, keeping the play in front of them and then hitting on the break. We have seen the counter-attacking styles of Mourinho flourish at various clubs. We learned that it was clear it wasn't just about how many times you passed but how you passed.

The game moves on. Everything now is measured and analysed. I will later discuss data and football scouting. At the top of the game the role of data analytics has become crucial in terms of analysing success in games and individual players' performances.

As a scout you need to think about what you believe is 'good football' and hence what makes a 'good

---

2   Stats from www.footballcritic.com

footballer'. If you are serious about the game and the scouting role you need to read some of the theories and ideas in this exciting new world of big data in football. It may well open your eyes to different ways of looking at the game and the players within it.

For myself, I will give you an example. I am fascinated by the discussions around what brings success in football. In my reading I often come across ideas that challenge the way I look at the game. For example, in the search for the holy grail of football analytics, the key indicator of success in games, having moved beyond the number of times you get the ball into the opponents' box, through the number of passes you make and so on, I came across 'packing'. This refers to measuring how many times a player plays a ball forward or dribbles a ball forward and how many opponents are bypassed in doing so. So, if your centre-back plays the ball forward to your striker and six opponents are bypassed, then both the centre-back and the striker get six positive 'packing' points.

I think this general concept originated in American sport but has been particularly developed in soccer by Stefan Reinartz, the former German international, and the Impect Group of analysts. That simple concept is the starting point for a whole series of data and assessment, indeed a whole way of looking at the game. For example, does your forward take up positions where a pass to him or for him can take out opponents in this way? Does your centre-back or full-back look first to play or move forward to take out opponents? Then again, when the other team have the ball; that is, when we are defending (wherever on the pitch the ball may be), does your play make it hard for the opposition to 'pack' players? Do we screen well? Do we close quickly and in such a manner as to reduce the chance of that forward pass?

The point is that in some 30 to 40 per cent of cases the team that amasses more 'packing' points wins the game. This overall approach to analysis has been adopted and developed further by top coaches such as Thomas Tuchel and seems to me an interesting way of looking at a game and the players within it.

As I reflected on this it did change the way I approached my scouting work. When doing a live detailed analysis of an individual player I will note down beforehand the key performance indicators that I want to measure. It might be passing success, or crosses, or shots or dribbles according to my view of what the key indicators are for a player in that position and at that age and level. I do this manually and live because for the most part I am not covering top senior games where the stats will be featured on various websites in real time! If you are covering a u14 academy game, for example, you are on your own – and you won't even have a team sheet!

With this in mind, I changed my approach. I could see how significant packing is. I don't have to believe it is the only stat worth having or even the single most important one – even the people developing and advocating it have a much more sophisticated view of the game than that. But it does seem to me to be an important one and a useful key or tool for identifying effective players.

I will talk later about different sorts of reporting and note-taking on players but, suffice here to say, if I am doing a detailed individual report on a player I will be ideally just focused on that player. If the ball is at the other end of the pitch, I am still watching my player. (I have learned when doing this sort of report to also make a note of the score, because many times I would be so focused on this player that if someone asked me afterwards what the score was, I did not always know, and that was embarrassing! However, it shows the strength of my focus and concentration, I suppose.)

Instead of just recording the number of passes made and the number that were successful (I have a simple little personal shorthand method I use) to give me a passing success rate and whether with right or left foot, I started to record whether they were forward or sideways or backwards as well. Ideally, I would like to record how many players were 'packed' by these passes, but it is so difficult to do that live. Even on video I believe it is still done manually, which must be very painstaking. I also began to note when forwards made themselves available for high-packing passes. We can see how an appreciation of the concept of packing has informed the way I look at the game and what I look for in players' performance. I do believe it has made my reporting more insightful and my analysis of players better focused.

My view of what constitutes a good performance has changed in some of the details over the years. The basics still hold true. Control, pass and move. Can we win the ball? But the details need to be varied depending on age and standard. What criteria you favour will be influenced by your view of the game and what constitutes a good player. That is fine. Having individual views and opinions is essential to the culture of a good recruitment team. (I will talk about the dangers of different forms of 'bias' later.)

But there also needs to be some common ground. A recruitment team needs a common language, so if we are talking about a 'good centre mid' we all know what we mean. You, as a scout, need to know what your club is looking for and what sorts of performance criteria it favours. It will help if you keep up with the ebb and flow of different views and ideas on the wider football stage. Fortunately, most of us will have the internet available to us and it is not difficult to keep reasonably up-to-date and informed. You just need to want to do it. This will give you the colour and context of the elephant you are looking for.

Follow the QR code here for me talking about what scouts look for:

Chapter Four

Position Profiles

AS PART of knowing exactly what our elephant looks like, it seems to me that we need to have a clear picture of what the ideal profile of each position might be – our ideal elephants. If we are looking at a left-back, for example, we need a clear picture of what a top left-back will be able to do – what they would look like. In this chapter I will set out an example of the attributes the ideal player would have in each position.

This is all my opinion. I do think each club should and often do develop their own set of profiles so their players, coaches and certainly scouts know the remit. Ideally, the scouts should be involved in developing those profiles. It is another facet of developing a common language in a club. I set these profiles out as examples of what they might look like and to demonstrate the concept of position profiles. If these examples do help you in your scouting or assessing of players, then so much the better, fill your boots!

I am looking here at mature first-team senior players. The profiles would need to be adjusted as you go back looking at younger and younger players. I would argue that at u9 to u11 you might not use any position profiles. You are developing footballers as opposed to right-backs or left-wingers or any other position. However, as the players get older, they do need to begin to demonstrate their suitability for specific positions, and by u18 they should be experts (for their age) at one position and, in my view, good performers in at least two other positions.

We know teams play different *systems*; that is, different ways of organising or setting up your team. In 3-4-3, for example, you do not have full-backs as such, but wing-backs, and the wider centre-backs need a slightly different set of abilities than if they were playing full-back or centre-back in a back four. I have tried to reflect a good range of positions that would feature in a back four, a back three, a midfield three, and forwards. There should be the positions here for 3-4-3, 5-3-2, 4-3-3, 4-2-3-1 and 4-4-2, which cover the most common systems, at least in the British game today.

The profiles cannot really reflect different *patterns of play*; that is, the ways teams play, such as playing out from the back, or playing a longer-ball game, or working the ball through the thirds of the pitch and so on. This would mean a huge number of positional profiles being required. We know that what a full-back is required to do in possession if his team is playing a long-ball, direct game will be different than if they are playing a passing game, progressing through the thirds. However, for these profile purposes I have had to try to summarise and crystallise the ideal attributes in these broad positions in these most common systems, rather than try to go through every possible pattern of play.

These are not exhaustive lists. They are just there to give an idea of the type of thing you might look for in the ideal players in the main positions. A lot more detail can be added but this begins to depend on exactly what way the coach wants a team to play and would then reflect the specific demands of different systems of play.

I think most coaches will tell their players what they want to do when they are in possession (i.e. attacking) and what they will want them to do when they are out of possession (i.e. defending), and I have reflected that in each position. Again, to be clear, let me repeat that I am considering we are attacking whenever and wherever we have the ball. For example, if our keeper has the ball in his hands, we are attacking. Conversely, if the opposition have the ball, wherever that is, then we are defending. So, if their keeper has the ball in his hands then we are defending. I have therefore shown attacking and defending attributes for each position.

In addition to the specific positional elements in the following pages, every player will need to show the individual attributes detailed in the player assessment model in Chapter Three: the technical, physical, psychological and tactical elements of the game.

Goalkeepers

In the modern game at the top level the goalkeepers are, of course, invariably over 190cm (6ft 3in) tall. There is the usual discussion as to whether a good smaller goalkeeper can make it to the top in the modern game, and there have been some exceptions that we know about. The goalkeeping coaches I have discussed this with have usually said that if there are good tall goalkeepers out there then why would you not go for them? Particularly in the Premier League, which is still a physically demanding one. It is also true that many aspects of the goalkeeping role – the command of the box, the taking of high crosses and the 'filling of the goal' – are aided by the bigger size. We can debate it all we like but the first question scouts are asked about goalkeepers is invariably 'how tall is he?' With this in mind, I will say that, at the very least, more coaches will be looking for the taller goalkeeper.

The whole requirement for goalkeepers changed dramatically with the introduction of the back-pass rule in 1992 after the football in the 1990 World Cup was widely criticised for being too defensive, with too much time-wasting. Suddenly goalkeepers were required to play out from the back and use their feet so much more. Prior to this they had only really kicked the ball from goal kicks or straight out of their hands. Now they had to control the ball from back passes. Gradually the positive side of this development became apparent, and it was acknowledged that goalkeepers could play out and become an extra defender and an extra passing option. This meant that goalkeepers' ability with the ball at their feet soon became a key element in assessing them. It is certainly a requirement these days, and at most levels goalkeepers must be comfortable in receiving the ball, manipulating it and then passing out, including being able to pass accurately over different distances to 'beat the press'; that is, bypass opponents who are pushing up and pressurising the defence, trying to win the ball back.

Attacking

- Able to receive and control the ball played to either foot in a variety of settings – at pace, in the air, bouncing ball.

- Comfortable with the ball at their feet – able to play out effectively with good tempo and accurate passes off either foot, even when under pressure.

- Able to find team-mates with their kicking by chipping and driving passes at pace to keep the game tempo up.

- Able to kick long and accurately off the ground and out of their hands to over the halfway line.

- Able to throw the ball at pace with accuracy over short and long distances (to the halfway line if necessary).

- Ready to make quick decisions about when and where to kick and execute this under pressure.

- Communicate with the team to aid organisation in possession.

- Be ready to take a positive starting position, adjusting it to the position of the ball so that, for example, when attacking in the opposition's last third, the goalkeeper is taking up an advanced starting position to act as 'sweeper keeper' as needed, well in advance of the edge of their penalty area.

Defending

- Good shot-stopping to either side, and able to move feet quickly and dive sharply.

- Good handling – whether catching shots or high balls cleanly, and able to palm balls away, when necessary, into safe areas.

- Comfortable in their area, taking up good positions, narrowing angles to reduce the amount of the goal seen by attackers, as needed.

- Good spring.

- Bravery – ready to go towards an attacker just about to have a shot and ready to go out one on one and dive in to claim the ball.

- Good body position, spreading the body well to maximise blocking of close shots.

- Good pace to be able to get out and claim a ball or challenge an opponent with sharpness and agility.

- Good, appropriate and timely communication to help organise the team's defensive movement and awareness and to make it clear when they are coming for a ball.

- Command of their penalty area with a physical presence and assurance giving confidence to team-mates.

- Mental toughness to be able to deal with mistakes and goals against.

- Absolute desire to keep the ball out of the net.

As the requirements for goalkeepers have changed over the years, our remit as scouts has adjusted as well. At the younger ages I think you are mainly looking for bravery and for the ability to keep the ball out of the net. This can often be seen in a real desire to make saves and defend the goal. Gradually you look for the technical development of a goalkeeper with better handling and better communication. Issues such as the starting position and their ability to play out gradually take on more importance. Then, of course, there is the issue that we have mentioned of height. This all makes scouting goalkeepers a difficult proposition for most general scouts. I have always appreciated listening to good goalkeeping coaches and learning what they look for in the technical ability of goalkeepers. It is becoming a specialist role. Specialist goalkeeping scouts are being used by the bigger clubs more and more and I think this will continue to be the case. Nevertheless, for the general scout, it is important to get an awareness of the basic technical requirements for a goalkeeper.

Centre-Backs

It is an old line that where centre-backs are concerned there are *cats* and *dogs*. *Cats* are the slinky, mobile, fluid footballer-type of centre-backs (think John

Stones), while the positive, old-fashioned centre-back, who attack the ball (think Harry Maguire) are the *dogs*. Ideally, you want a combination of both (think Thiago Silva), but we indeed seem to have a generation of centre-backs who are happier dropping off and 'sweeping' than marking an opponent and have often come through their academy careers usually only facing one striker between two centre-backs. These 'cats' do not want to mark and will pass on their forward to be marked by someone else wherever they can. Alternatively, if you want to be playing out from the back, some 'dogs' cannot pass the ball out at all well.

Most head coaches want height and some aerial ability in their centre-backs. They all must have pace and, as a general theme, we have noticed that as forwards have become more mobile over the years, so have defenders to counteract them. If a head coach is going to play a high line in their back four, they really need to have defenders who have tactical discipline and can deal with the big spaces that are going to be in behind them. Many centre-backs who are not quite as quick would be very nervous about leaving that sort of space and will naturally tend to drop off. So once again we find that we need to know what sort of system our club is employing to find the centre-backs that suit that system. Where younger players are concerned we are looking for an ideal combination of pace, height, ability on the ball and, of course, the crucial element of being able as a defender to win the ball.

Attacking

- Ability to play out from the back with either foot, short or long, and being comfortable on the ball.
- Comfortable playing out on either side.
- Good passing range, including hitting driven diagonals accurately to switch play.
- Ability to bring the ball out of defence, 'breaking the lines', creating overloads in midfield and positively developing attacking play.
- Able to contribute to attacking set pieces and threaten goal/score goals.

Defending

- Ability to effectively attack the ball and win it fairly on the ground and in the air.
- Good spring to make defensive headers.
- Ability to head away safely.
- Able to jockey, win the ball and make the right decisions of when to tackle and when to hold up play.

- Quick enough to be able to turn and defend balls played down the sides.
- Good reading of the game to cover and keep a good defensive line and shape.
- Good communication to help organise and coordinate defence.

Centre-Backs (in a back three)

All the above attributes of a centre-back plus some others:

Defensively

- Able to go out wide and defend in exposed wing positions as a full-back would.
- Knows when to step into midfield to create overloads.

If a head coach wants to play a back three, then all sorts of other permutations and considerations come into play. For example, it is notable now that the teams playing a back three will often want to capitalise on the fact that one of these will be the spare man in many cases. This means that one of the back three can move into midfield as we have seen recently with John Stones at Manchester City or Steve Basham at Sheffield United. Consequently, if a head coach wants this sort of capacity in a player, we would again be looking at tactical understanding, and it would place a premium on being able to play virtually as a midfielder at times as John Stones, for example, is able to do.

Right/Left-Back

There is a big difference between those full-backs who can play comfortably in a back four and those who really need to be wing-backs. I always felt that Marcos Alonso, now at Barcelona, fell into this category when he was playing for Chelsea. He was very effective as a left wing-back and played a key part in Antonio Conte's Premier League-winning team, but I was never as comfortable with him when he was playing in a back four. I was not convinced about his one-to-one defending and his pace on the turn, but as a wing-back going forward he was very effective and could attack the back post well.

In the modern game there seem to be relatively few full-backs who can happily play in a back four or as a wing-back. I think Andy Robertson of Liverpool and Scotland is one of these exceptions and, for me, he is currently probably the best all-round left-back in the Premier League. Reece James of Chelsea would obviously be a strong candidate. He can also play in a back four or as a wing-back and he's one of the top players in his position in the world, as is Robertson.

Head coaches will sometimes want the full-backs even in a back four to be good at getting forward and providing some width. So immediately in these cases you are looking at requirements of pace, ability to beat opposition players and crossing and passing skills. This will particularly be the case if the teams are playing with a narrow midfield. Once again, if we look at Pep Guardiola's Manchester City and Mikel Arteta's Arsenal, we can see how they will often get a full-back to push into midfield to create the extra man there, and leave three at the back when in possession. All these differing requirements from head coaches will affect what the ideal full-back looks like.

Attacking

- Able to go forward with pace when there is attackable space in front of them and get crosses in.
- Able to receive the ball from the goalkeeper or other defenders and play out comfortably.
- Able to 'open up' and go forward on the outside and inside.
- Able to combine well with midfielders.
- Able to hit positive forward passes, in behind the defence when necessary.

- Knows when to go forward and when to hold the line.
- Takes throw-ins effectively, quickly and at a good tempo.

Defending

- Able to win the ball in tackles and then keep possession.
- Good overall one-on-one defending skills in terms of body position and effectiveness.
- Good pace to be able to defend in wide areas.
- Good mobility and agility to compete against quick forwards.
- Good reading of the game to know when to close up to the nearest centre-back and cover ground and when to press the opponent.

Players who become full-backs when they are senior players often start in academy football in different positions. Reece James started his career as a forward when he first came into Chelsea at age seven or eight but then played in midfield before converting to a full-back at around 14 years of age. Ashley Cole was a striker when a young boy and became one of the best left-backs in the world. Academies often find that they have a lot of midfield players at younger ages, as in many cases talented young players will play in midfield and be all over the pitch at the grassroots level. Consequently, it is not surprising that those players settle down into other positions as they get older. If we are looking for a specialist full-back though, either for a player in the older academy ages or as a senior player, then we need to be aware of all the various demands the different systems will put upon that player as set out above.

Right/Left Wing-Back

All the above attributes for right/left-backs plus these others:

Attacking

- Able to take on opponents with tricks and/ or pace, beat an opponent and take the play forward.
- Able to hit accurate crosses high and low on the run at pace.
- Able to get in at the far post and attack the goal.

Defending

- Extra stamina to get up and down the wing, getting back to help defend as needed then able to get forward to join the attack.

Wingers will often find themselves being played as wing-backs and this can work very well, as it did, for example, with Victor Moses when Antonio Conte moved him to right wing-back in his Premier League-winning team. I think it is becoming more of a specialist position though. I do think from a scouting point of view and a player development point of view that the ideal is a full-back who can play both in a back four and as a wing-back, or a winger who can also play as a wing-back. This versatility will mean these players can be useful in almost whatever system the head coach is going to use.

Defensive Centre-Midfield

Not every system will use a defensive mid – a 'Makelele' or a 'No.6', but when teams play 4-2-3-1, the two No.6s must have a lot of the attributes set out here too. We do see centre-backs who can make the transition into playing as a defensive midfielder. Eric Dier comes to mind. It is a position that requires a lot of tactical understanding for a player to take up the right positions and shield the back four, and even block passing lines to the opposition forwards.

If the defensive mid has an attacking player to pick up, perhaps this might be someone playing as the No.10 in a 4-2-3-1 or a 4-4-2 with a diamond midfield. In those cases, defensively it is a relatively straightforward position.

The role has most often been seen as a defensive one in essence, and that was how Claude Makelele played it under Jose Mourinho at Chelsea when the role became linked to his name. However, we have also seen players such as Andrea Pirlo, who are deep-lying playmakers, play in similar areas yet play a different type of role.

These are more of what the term 'quarterback' is usually applied to, someone who acts as a 'pivot' for building attacks and developing play with good passing skills.

So there may be different types of players required as a defensive mid or No.6, and again we come back to the point that as a scout you will need to know how they are being utilised to identify the ideal candidates. Even if it is a more defensive role it does seem to me that it is extremely important that the player in this role can pass well and begin attacks and knows when to push up and make an extra man as an attack develops. Some head coaches will deploy someone in this position purely as a defensive shield for the back four, and if there are full-backs pushing on, then the defensive mid can be a third player who drops back into a back line at times.

Attacking

- Able to receive the ball on either foot in tight areas and keep possession.
- Able to pass well and positively, passing forward wherever possible, short and long on either side.
- Makes themselves available to receive the ball, find space to do so and support play.
- Reads the game well to move up and around as needed.

Defending

- Able to win the ball and break up attacks.
- Able to shield the back four and position well to intercept.
- Able to cover ground quickly and press effectively.
- Able to win headers and defend longer balls as needed.

Many times, when I have had young players coming in for a trial game or a series of sessions, I have asked a player what their best position is, and they say defensive mid, and this does concern me a bit. Many teams play without that role, as we have seen. I would much rather a young player say to me that they can play as a '6' or an '8', and I do think that flexibility is needed.

Centre-Midfield

To some extent the centre-midfielders, the No.8s as we know them, should be able to do what the defensive midfielder does plus add the further attributes set out overleaf. Even then we know that there are different types of centre-midfielders. For me, the ideal is a Roy Keane or Patrick Vieira, who are very mobile and very effective in breaking up play but can also use the ball well and attack with it. Players who can only do the defensive or the attacking parts of the game are less desirable.

We see these differences in a lot of current teams, so you might have a Declan Rice, who was more defensive perhaps at West Ham, although pushes further forward now at Arsenal. I think all-round footballers such as Kevin De Bruyne, who is more of an attacking midfielder and can also play as a No.10 or as one of the front three, have shown that they have the defensive capabilities to be considered as an all-round centre-midfielder, as have Luka Modrić and Toni Kroos of Real Madrid. Jude Bellingham has been a more attacking midfielder but, as he is maturing, he again shows all-round ability. Top midfielders in the past such as Steven Gerrard and Frank Lampard also showed high standards in both aspects of the game and I think this is what we look for when we are scouting for these positions.

Attacking

- Able to pass quickly and accurately off either foot on either side and play at a good tempo.
- Good enough 'engine' to get up and down in midfield.
- Able to read the game to know when to go forward and when to stay back.
- Capacity to run ahead of the ball when needed.
- Ability to score goals from midfield, from long range and/or timing runs into the box, joining the attack.
- Ability to command midfield, dictating the pace and tempo of the play.

Defending

- Able to pick up opponents, mark effectively and track runners.
- Energy to make good recovery runs.
- Ability to win the ball, break up play and keep possession.
- Know when to block forward passes to opponents' forwards, thus acting as a shield.

Attacking Centre-Mid/Inside-Forward

Again, not every system will have a '10' as you would find in a 4-2-3-1 perhaps, but with systems like 3-4-3 or the box midfields we often see teams deploying two No.10s or 'inside-forwards'. The problem has often been that this is sometimes seen as a 'free role' in that an attacking player might feel they have the licence to drift where they want. If you say a player can go anywhere, they sometimes end up going nowhere! The position needs discipline and tactical understanding. The creative attacking side of the role must not completely overshadow the responsibilities the No.10s have to defend, picking up key opponents, stopping defenders breaking out, and dropping back if necessary to block out space in midfield or go forward and join a higher press. So, while the position may conjure up images of Maradona or Bergkamp, contemporary No.10s such as Phil Foden, James Maddison and Mason Mount understand the broader nature of the modern role.

Attacking

- Ability to find space and make themselves available to receive the ball and develop attacks.
- Good receiving skills, able to take the ball on the half-turn and fluidly go forwards with it.
- Ability to beat opponents and create scoring opportunities for themself and others.

- Able to see and execute the threaded pass in behind or alongside the defence to play forwards in.
- Good movement off the ball to create opportunities to play for themself or others.
- Able to finish and score goals.

Defending

- Good at transitions and ready to defend as needed.
- Ability to read the game to pick up and mark and track back as needed.
- Able to press effectively with good game understanding to know when to press and when to sit off, according to team pattern of play.

Young players who say their best position is as a No.10 or attacking midfielder often have these images of a creative player drifting about. So as a scout you are looking for good game understanding in anyone playing the position, as set out above. Also, for young players, as with the defensive midfield role, it can be a limitation if this is the only role they can play, as not every team will use a No.10. From a scouting point of view, you might see a striker who you think may not have the absolute pace or physicality you might look for in a No.9 but you may feel they would work well behind the striker. The same can apply to wingers – if you see they can move either way, maybe it is not so important that they are not absolute speed merchants, and perhaps they could do better as a No.10.

Right/Left Wing

There is a fashion for 'inverted' wingers; that is, left-footers playing on the right wing and vice-versa. It is quite rare to see a right-footed winger go outside a left-back and get crosses in now, although it can still be very effective. So, we see Bukayo Saka of Arsenal or Cole Palmer of Chelsea as left-footed players coming off the right, or Jack Grealish of Manchester City as a right-footed player playing off the left. Regardless of which side or which foot, the following attributes are needed for all top wingers, whether in a 4-4-2 or a 4-3-3.

Attacking

- Ability to take on and beat opponents on the outside and inside.
- Pace enough to get away from defenders.
- Ability to cross the ball at pace, driven and lofted accurately and early into dangerous areas.
- Good finishing, able to score goals.

- Good reading of the game to know when to stay out wide and give width and when to join in closer to the striker(s).

- Good game understanding to position themselves on different lines than their full-backs, and if they are required to get wide then get really wide, with 'chalk on their boots'!

Defending

- Willingness to track back and defend and stop defenders playing out.

- Energy and ability to press and close down effectively.

When scouting a winger, again you need to know what type of player is required – a real out-and-out wide player with pace or more of a No.10 playing in the inside-forward channel.

Striker

The ideal striker can drop off and link play and go in behind with pace (think Robert Lewandowski, Didier Drogba, Harry Kane). There are not many that can do both and score goals. That is why they are so prized! Virtually every team at every level will find room for a top striker. There are different types of strikers in practice: a target man who is good in the air, good at holding the ball up and playing others in (think Olivier Giroud, for example) or a speedster looking to get in behind (think Jamie Vardy).

Attacking

- Ability to score goals – to finish well from close range and longer range, with either foot and with headers.
- Pace and power.
- Able to drop off and hold up the ball, using their body, showing good receiving skills at all levels, including with their chest, shielding the ball and linking play.
- Able to get regularly into the golden area in front of goal to be available for chances.
- Ready to run in behind to stretch defences.
- Able to vary movement with curved runs, creating and finding space in the key area in front of the goal and working across the line.
- Able to link with team-mates, passing the ball to create opportunities for others and develop attacks, using either foot or head.
- Able to play as a single striker and as one of two strikers; that is, leading the line as needed, and also linking and working off team-mates.

Defending

- Able and willing to press effectively and close down opponents to help win the ball as near the opponents' goal as possible.
- Willingness to work to cover and track back as needed and stop defenders from having time to play the ball out easily.
- Capacity to help play their part and defend set pieces well.

You will spend a lot of time as a scout watching strikers. Partly this is because just about every team, as I have said, would take a top striker if they could find one, and because they catch the eye. If you can find a young player – say around 13 or 14, who has that instinctive movement to create space for themselves and can also finish coolly, then that is a real find and a great start. Most players will need to be coached to learn that, and not all young strikers take it on board even then. Goalscorers come in all shapes and sizes and will always be of interest.

For further info on 'What Makes a Top Striker' check out my video here:

Chapter Five

Reporting on a Player

AS A scout our principal working environment is the touchline or the stands, be they in the local park or the San Siro. Watching players and assessing them is what we do. However, if we do not communicate our assessment, our work is pointless. Reporting is how we showcase and present our work; it is actually our *product*.

The ways we report and the media we use inevitably have changed and will continue to do so. In modern times we may have apps we can use, or we might report through remote online systems straight on to databases. It will, of course, vary according to the type of scouting we are doing and who we are doing it for in the sense of the level of the club we are reporting for, in many cases.

In grassroots scouting – looking at players on the local parks and recreation grounds – the reporting is often quite basic as you are usually looking at a lot of players and looking for something that catches your eye. This is often termed as *scanning*. If you pick the right venue you might be able to watch a whole series of games at different ages and different levels. That would certainly be the case at the tournaments.

Most grassroots scouts have their own system of noting players of interest, whether in the proverbial trusty notebook or on their phones. Some keep their own database or spreadsheet of players so they can track who they need to see again and so on.

Many academies now provide their grassroots scouts with apps that enable them to log where they have been, how many players they have seen, what the game and league or cup was, at what age and to note any players of interest. This data can then be managed centrally on a database and can also provide scout activity reports for coordinators as well as helping in tracking and cross-referencing players of interest.

For academy scouting – that is, the scouting of players in other academy teams – the level of reporting tends to be of a somewhat higher standard and more structured. Clubs may use an available commercial scouting system – Scout 7, for example – or have developed their own. These are all ways of getting information on players and an assessment of players into a database that allows tracking and coordination.

For most clubs' requirements, you will be making notes pitchside and then transferring them on to whichever database system is used later. Some clubs do have tablet or phone apps that allow direct input from pitchside, but these are not widely used yet.

Thumbnails

There will usually be two levels of report on a player. The first will be a relatively brief 'player assessment report', which we can term here a 'thumbnail'. In this type of report you are setting out some simple information on a player based on what you see:

1. **Match Details:** Who were the teams? What date? What was the venue? What were the conditions? What was the score? How did the game unfold? What formations did the teams use? If you are doing a series of thumbnails from one particular game – as is often the case – you can cut and paste this first section to head every report. You may ask why it needs to be on every individual report. The answer is that most scouting database systems allow for the looking up of reports on individual players (as well as all reports on a particular game). So if each individual thumbnail on a player from various

games is complete in and of itself, then it will be a more comprehensive picture when they are brought together in a list of thumbnails.

2.**Description:** What does the player look like? This is important, because if another scout goes to see the player (or if you do again) they need to know what they are looking for. What shirt number? This can, of course, vary from game to game, but many academies operate squad numbers, so within a season a player's shirt number may be consistent. It is also of help if you manage to get hold of video coverage of the game at a later date. What position(s) did he play? It is important to log what positions a player is used in. Academies may be putting players out of their comfort zone by playing in different and sometimes unfamiliar positions, but largely you would get an idea of where coaches see them as playing.

3.**Strengths:** What did the player do well? We so often focus on what a player cannot do but it is important to get some sort of picture of what they *can* do. I accept that sometimes for some players this is difficult to identify. You might be reporting on a lot of players – if you are doing thumbnails then you probably will be – and some players just do not stand out. However, you can try to look for some physical attribute or something positional or technical.

4. **Weaknesses:** What was not so good? Again some players may just be 'okay' and doing nothing particularly poorly. This is where your observation skills come in and the devil may well be in the detail.

5. **Performance Rating:** How did the player do on the day? Each club may have their rating system – maybe A/B/C/D, or scores out of five or out of ten. Whatever system is used it is vital that all scouts agree on what each score means so there is some consistency of rating. This may seem an obvious thing to say but you might be surprised at the number of clubs where this common understanding of exactly what their own ratings mean is not strong enough. If it is about *performance*, you are rating that player in that game. So if a striker scores a hat-trick and does all they can do in that game against that opposition, then in my view you would rate their performance as very good, however your system expresses that. Players can only perform on the day against whoever is in front of them. This does not mean you are saying they are for you.

6. **Potential Rating:** How do you judge the player in terms of their future potential? We are often looking at players to try to assess what they will do in the future and, as we have discussed, this is naturally difficult. But we need to differentiate

between *performance* (what the player did on the day in that game) and *potential* (what they might be in future). Again this needs careful discussion across a scouting team, so everyone is on the same page as to the different scores and their meaning. Are we looking at potential in six months? Or six years? We need to all agree. We need that common language.

7. **Action:** What next? This could range from 'dismiss' or 'disregard' through to 'watch again' or 'get senior staff to watch urgently', depending on each club's recruitment team structure and systems, or maybe even 'sign' if you are that confident.

These we can call *thumbnails*; that is, a brief picture of a player. One might look something like this:

Example Thumbnail

Saturday, 28 October 2022. X Rovers u18s v Y City u18s. Academy u18 League. X Training ground, good grass pitch, sunny morning.

X Rovers u18s hosted Y City u18s and were much the better team. Playing a 4-3-3 throughout, Rovers passed the ball better, were more positive and had more possession. They were 2-0 up at half-time and went on to win 5-1. City, playing a 4-4-2, which was changed at half-time to a 3-5-2 to try to match Rovers in midfield, were a younger team with four u16s playing and struggled to cope with the stronger, more physical Rovers team, although they did threaten occasionally on the break.

Charlie Smith – white, slim, short dark hair, 5ft 8in, right-footed but used left, u16, wearing No.17 – played as right-wing for Y City and played 80 minutes before being subbed. He showed good pace, good touch and control with his preferred right foot and was ready to take players on and kept working hard. He scored the City G1 on 56 minutes, latching on to a long clearance, getting in behind the Rovers defence and finishing smartly right-footed. He was a bit lightweight and was outmuscled at times by the older stronger opponents and tended to always want to take the opponent on the outside (i.e. his right side), which was a bit predictable. He faded physically and it was not a surprise he was subbed later in the game.

Performance: 6/10 Potential: 8/10

Charlie is a lively u16 with real pace. It would be good to see him in his age group so **Action = Watch Again**.

Some clubs will require thumbnails on a lot of players in a game, as I have said – maybe all the players from one team on the basis they are building up information on all players. This is a demanding task as it could mean around 14 reports, including substitutes, for example, but it does deliver a lot of data for clubs and a lot of background on players. This will require a lot of notes, whether in a notebook or on your phone! Other clubs will only require scouts to pick out the best three players – maybe the best three from each team. Other clubs may only want reports on players that stand out. However many reports clubs seek, if they are initial summary reports, they will tend to be thumbnails of some sort, as shown in the example above.

If you had never seen Charlie Smith before but were asked to watch him for your next match assignment, then reading the report above would give you some idea of what to look for – remember at a lot of academy games, as we shall discuss later, you do not get team sheets. Some clubs do not want to share other scouts' reports with their scouts so as not to affect their judgement. Overall, however, I personally feel that a club is best served by a culture that supports different opinions and encourages scouts to make up their own minds but makes the job simpler by sharing some background on players, where possible, in advance. So, in this way, a club or an individual scout can build up a series of brief pictures of players – our 'thumbnails'. These will help the coordinators – or again, the scout, depending on the system a club uses – to identify which players are worth following up on and watching again, perhaps in more detail.

Sometimes we must make up our minds on a player on one showing. This is not ideal at all. Perhaps we learn that the player is just about to sign for another club, or whatever the circumstance might be. These are the exceptions that prove the rule, however, because the rule must be that unless you absolutely cannot avoid it, then you need to make big decisions on a player based on more than one viewing and ideally involving more than one scout.

Bringing a player in on trial is a big commitment of resources for a club (we will discuss later how trials work at clubs). However, seriously looking to buy or sign a player is a big commitment at all levels. It is not, of course, just about a possible transfer fee. It is about the commitment you will need to make as a club – perhaps taking up a chunk of the playing budget, of coaching resources or taking up a squad shirt and thereby potentially excluding other players. Decisions have consequences.

For example, you might be watching a u14 for an academy. If you believe your club should sign the player you are effectively saying they will need to give him a two-year registration covering the u15 and u16s, as it is a two-year commitment. If you are suggesting the club pays compensation for the player, then the club will want to know that the player is going to be worth a scholarship at 16, and that is a further two-year commitment. By then a top player will have an agent on board and they will want a commitment to a future first-year pro deal. So your saying 'yes' to a u14 signing may mean you believe your club has to commit to a five-year programme in practice. This is not always the case but it illustrates the point that, even away from the big-money headline signings, a relationship with a player is invariably a commitment of resources, and these are usually finite.

Let's imagine you are scouting for a non-league club at a decent level – say Step 3. Your club needs a left-back and you think you have found what is needed when you watch a player in one game a couple of steps below. You find out the player is non-contract so there will be no fee involved, just a formal seven-day notice of approach, and your club can legally approach them to see whether they will sign. No pressure then? Or is there?

If you sign this player, they will presumably need paying and that will take a slice of the budget. Fair enough. However, at Step 3 your club might want first-team players to all be on contract and you might need to offer him longer than just through to the end of the season. He might get a season and a half on contract. So you might be recommending to your club that they block off a bigger chunk of resources than it at first appears. Given a limited budget, if you sign one left-back you will not want to be signing another – your budget wouldn't wear it! So is this the *best* left-back you can get? Are you happy to decide based on just one game?

You need to watch him a couple of times at least – maybe against different levels of opponents, maybe home and away ideally. Players can have good or bad games for all sorts of reasons. Everyone has off days – even scouts! Ideally you want to watch a player multiple times, but you do not always get the opportunity. So you need to be sure, and the best way to be sure is to see the player over a series of games yourself and get other opinions too. Scouting nowadays is a team activity built upon combining individual opinions.

Ideally, clubs will have a recruitment structure and levels of decision-making. That will, of course, vary according to resources and levels of clubs, but getting further opinions is not a sign of weakness in a scout, rather a sign of good professionalism.

At a top club with a good scouting structure, it is not uncommon to seek around ten reports from at least five different scouts to maximise the validity of any scouting recommendation. The more games and the more scouts, the more valid the ratings are. So at the top level, the recruitment analysts will often be presenting data from the scouting database that shows not just the average rating of a player but with some indication of the validity of such ratings.

Sometimes decisions are made on other criteria and via other processes. At one big club I know, the head of recruitment analysis had a top team of bright analysts working on a database showing the assessments of a further team of top professional scouts. They all worked really hard to present the top ten candidates for any given position and criteria the club asked for. One lunchtime, in a transfer window, he literally bumped into a top striker from another club in his club canteen wearing his club's training kit. When he asked the head of recruitment what the player was doing there, the guy shrugged and said,

'I don't know. The first I heard was this morning. The chairman told me he signed. That was that. He'd come available and the chairman decided we would sign him.' He was not on their top ten list of strikers. They were not even targeting a striker. This was a multi-million-pound signing that had not been informed at all by any of the excellent scouting, data and research teams the club had set up. And they say it's a funny game?

On another occasion I met the senior goalkeeping coach for a Premier League club that had just paid a lot of money for a relatively unknown goalkeeper. I asked what he thought of him. He looked away briefly then turned back to me. 'I was asked for a list of the top ten keepers I thought we should sign,' he said, then looked away again. 'He wasn't on it. Next thing I know, I'm told we have signed him.'

So sometimes decisions are made based on other criteria than a solid scouting set-up. In the modern game they are often explained by the agents who circulate around the owners and key decision-makers within the big clubs on the international scene, so often normal decision-making routes are bypassed. Sometimes, of course, this might be for good reasons and sometimes they may work out. Sometimes they just beggar belief.

However, these are the exceptions. The *recruitment* practices of clubs – particularly at the top level – would be the subject of another book. Where the *scouting* of players is concerned – the assessment of players – then it is logical to try to get a series of views and to involve other trusted opinions wherever possible at all levels of the game, from grassroots right to the top if it is feasible.

Portraits

Going back to our reporting then, let's assume we want to report thoroughly on an individual player. For the sake of an example, let's assume there have been a few thumbnails done and a couple of scouts have liked the look of a player, so it is decided that the next viewing will be an in-depth assessment of this individual player. Or it might be the case that a player has been flagged up to the club as worth a close look and they send you along. Or you might have had a preliminary look at a player, liked him and now want to do a more in-depth individual assessment.

What is now required is what we might term a 'portrait' of a player – a real examination of an individual performance in a specific game. This is much more in-depth than the thumbnail. As mentioned you might do a dozen thumbnails from a game; however, you will only do one *portrait* per game (perhaps plus one or two thumbnails if other players also stand out).

When you do a portrait you are focusing essentially on this one player. If the ball is down the other end of the pitch you are still watching your individual player. (I must say, when doing this type of in-depth individual report – which is my favourite type of scouting – this is one of those times when I have to remind myself to make a note of the score, as I have been focused on my portrait.)

Before we get to the report itself we must think about what data we want to have to help us compile the report. We can do some background research on a player and find out what we can. Then we need to consider what position they are likely to play and what we as a club seek in that position (obviously tailored for age). So, we go back to our club 'position profiles' – featured in Chapter Four – and think about what we need to assess. Again, we need to know our elephant.

Let's assume for this example that we are going to follow up on Charlie Smith, our u16 winger we saw playing for Y City and who we did a thumbnail on and gave a 6/10 performance rating but an interesting 8/10 potential rating. We are now going to see him play in a u16 cup game and have decided to do a portrait report on him. We know he often plays up in the u18s but, given it is a cup game, Y City are putting out their strongest team and our sources tell us he will be playing in his own age group.

Our position profiles (which we may well have on our phone for easy reference, of course) tell us our ideal fully formed winger needs the following attributes:

Attacking

- Ability to take on and beat opponents on the outside or inside.
- Pace enough to get away from defenders.
- Ability to cross the ball at pace, driven and lofted accurately and early into dangerous areas.
- Good finishing, able to score goals.
- Good reading of the game to know when to stay out wide and give width and when to join in closer to the striker(s).

Defending

- Willingness to track back and defend and stop defenders playing out.
- Energy and ability to press and close down effectively.

So we might decide that the key performance indicators (KPIs) that will tell us whether our target is doing what we are seeking are:

- Dribbling
- Crossing
- Finishing
- Tackling
- Pressing

Therefore, in our notebook or phone, we are going to record the number of times our Charlie Smith does these things and whether they are successful. (I would also usually report on pass success, noting forward passing and also attempts at goal.) This will all help us build data for possible use in our report.

If you are reporting on a professional-level game, you may not have to bother collecting this data yourself as there are websites that provide this sort of individual performance data free or for a subscription. For the sake of our example though, we have a game where you are going to have to do it manually yourself.

Most scouts who work in this way soon develop their own shorthand way of noting this KPI data quickly and effectively. I have, so for passing, for example, I put the heading 'PASSING' down and take the player's strongest foot (in Charlie's case – right) as the default, so I just need to note the variations from that – when he uses his left. So the written entry under passing might look like this:

```
    L       L L      L
FSSFBBFBBBFFBBSSSF//FBBSBBFFFSFBFBBSF
x  x  x  x     x x        x   x
```

What will this tell me?

- The first line is the number of passes Charlie made with his left – all the others I know are with his default right.

- The second line is the general direction of the passes themselves – F = Forward, B = Back, S = Sideways. The two lines // show half-time.

- The third line notes the unsuccessful passes – those that went astray.

From this simple bit of data collection I can tell the following:

- Passing success rate (with either foot).
- Passing intent – percentage Forward/ Backward/Sideways (again with either foot).
- Number of passes overall and in either half.

So for Charlie I can record from my notes that he did the following in this game:

- Made 35 passes, 18 in the first half, 17 in the second.

- Overall, 27 were successful (77%), 13 were forward (37%) and of these forward passes eight were successful (61%).
- 31/35 passes were with the right foot (89%) but of the four (11%) made with the left, only two were successful (50%).

I will break down the other KPIs into an easily measurable and practical notation so I can get some data on the number of crosses, how good he was at getting past opponents, whether he tackled back effectively and so on. I think you can begin to see why compiling an effective portrait report on a player is an intensive and absorbing task. There is a lot for you to do during the game, so it is vital to develop a way of easily recording the data you want without overburdening yourself so much that your nose is buried in your notebook and you miss half the action. This is a common challenge for a thorough scout.

You will need to limit the number of KPIs you are reporting on. I have found six is about the maximum I can do well and get all the info I need at the same time. You could consider speaking into your phone and recording your comments by voice, and I know one or two scouts who favour that. But in a stand where you have been seated by the host club alongside several other scouts, you might not want to do that and be overheard!

I might not actually want to use all this data in the report when I come to writing it. The data is only as useful in as much as it informs the assessment of this player in this game. I will not include it in the final report just for its own sake or to show how busy I have been!

In addition to the data collection for the KPIs, I need to organise my information so I can report on the following – much the same as the thumbnail headings:

- Match Summary
- Player Description
- Overall Player Performance
- Strengths
- Weaknesses
- Overall Assessment
- Action

Our portrait report therefore might look something like this:

Example Portrait

Wednesday, 15 November. Y City vs Z Rangers, u16 Midweek Cup, Y City Training

Ground Stadium, good grass pitch, dry cold night, floodlights.

Match Summary:

Y City u16s played Z Rangers u16s in the u16 Midweek Cup. The match ended 3-2 to Z Rangers. Y City, playing 4-2-3-1, passed the ball around well and dominated possession in the first half but lacked punch. Z Rangers, playing a narrow 4-4-2, which moved to a more attacking 4-2-4 on the break, defended well, kept Y City in front of them and then hit with pace and intent. The competitive game was 1-1 at half-time, then Z Rangers scored two quick goals to lead 3-1. Y City had all the ball in the last 15 minutes, pressing and more positive, and did manage to get one goal back.

Performance Summary:

Charlie Smith – white, short dark hair, about 5ft 8in, right-footed but did use left, wearing No.7, played right wing for Y City, although moved to the left wing at the start of the second half before returning to right wing for the last 15 minutes. He scored City's second goal, late in the game, getting in behind the Rangers defence and firing a fierce right-foot shot across the GK. He showed good touch and technique, particularly on his preferred right foot, and good pace with and without the ball, but lacked intensity. He spectated far too much and only really came alive when the ball was near him. He passed the ball well, mostly over shorter distances but lacked positivity in his passing, opting for safe, easy sideways and backwards passes when City needed more punch and penetration.

Strengths:

+ *Technique:*

Charlie showed good touch and control, particularly on his stronger right foot, and passed the ball well, although mostly over shorter distances and again mostly with his right foot. Overall he made 35 passes, 18 in the first half and 17 in the second. This reflects that he had periods when he drifted out of the game. When he did get on the ball his passing was mostly accurate – 27/35 were successful (77%), but he tended to lack ambition – only 13 were forwards (37%) and of these eight were successful (61%). He tended to pass for the sake of it at times, and when he did try to be more positive, as the stats show, he was less successful. He mostly used his right – 31/35 passes were with the right foot (89%), but of the four (11%) made with the left only two were successful (50%).

He was good at going at defenders when he chose to do so – he attempted seven dribbles and five of these were successful, begging the question as to why he did not try this more often. He made five crosses, three of which were successful, although these mostly came when he did take on the full-back on the outside and cross from wide areas.

He had two shots at goal – the first in the first half skimmed the bar from 18 metres and the second was his goal, around 74 minutes, when on a rare occasion he was played in behind the defence and he ran on to fire home well from just inside the box on the right-hand side and accurately across the GK.

+ *Pace & Movement:*

Charlie showed he had pace with and without the ball, able to drive past defenders on the few occasions when he opted to do so. For his goal, for example, he was played in with a ball over the full-back and he outstripped his opponent for pace, taking one touch then fired home. He moved well, was light on his feet and agile, and could accelerate away from opponents.

Weaknesses:

- Intensity:

Charlie was too casual at times, watching the game go by unless the ball was nearby. He rarely adjusted his position on transitions, for example, unless the ball was nearby. He rarely worked back with any conviction and made only two tackles, only one of which was successful. He seemed to be going through the motions, playing back in his own age group when he has often been playing up recently. He rarely communicated with team-mates and was often not engaged in the game and did not appear to be fully focused at times. When the ball was at the other end of the pitch he was often walking slowly back or standing still. He rarely showed any urgency in movement off the ball, and his recovery runs – when he did make them – were not as quick as his forward running when the ball was near him!

- Negative Play:

Charlie's passing was too often just safe and rarely helped open the opposition either by incisive passing or by playing to his strength – running with the ball – and going at and beyond the defender. He would too often receive the ball and then just pass back to the full-back behind him or an easy lay-off to the nearest midfielder.

Performance Rating: 5/10

Potential:

Charlie has pace and ability. He is athletic and moves well. He has regularly been playing up and this may have contributed to his over-casual approach in this game in his own age group. He lacked engagement and intensity in his play and was too casual too often. However, when he did put everything together he showed he could hurt the opposition with that pace and ability. The query on him would be whether he could be encouraged to develop the necessary intensity or whether this is now a character trait that is ingrained and part of his personality. Overall he would not get a place in our u16s as right-winger above xxxxxz xxxxxx and we also have xxxx xxxx in the year below who can match Charlie's pace and has a more positive attitude.

Potential Rating: 6/10

Action:

Charlie has ability and is a good athlete but lacks application throughout a game at this stage. As such, and given he is not in a priority position for us, I would recommend we watch him again later in the season but that he is not a target player for us at this stage.

So in this *portrait* report, we have again described the player, noting appearance and shirt number – for the same reason we did in the *thumbnail* – to help the next scout who reports on him to be able to recognise the target. We have summarised the game to give us some context and captured Charlie's overall performance. We have looked at strengths and weaknesses in some depth using the data we have collected manually and used examples from the game to illustrate these facets, finishing with a performance rating. Then we can look at where Charlie fits in terms of potential, and this is where our knowledge of our own squads is so vital because we identify where Charlie might or might not fit with us. We can then rate his potential and identify the next action (if any).

I would argue that, having done a thumbnail and a portrait of a player, our immediate work with that player is done. If our reports are positive it is up to our club's scouting schedulers – whoever they may be – to get Charlie watched by another scout. This is because we must be aware of *confirmation bias*. (We will look at the range of biases that confront a scout later, in Chapter Twelve.) For now, let's say this is the natural tendency to look for information that supports a view we already have. If we have made our minds up about a player then at subsequent viewings we often seek to find arguments to support or reinforce our original view. A top scout must develop the ability to keep an open mind and just being aware of possible confirmation bias is a big help to counteract it. However, the general point is that after a certain number of viewings it is pointless having the same pair of eyes checking out the same player.

There can, though, be reasons to do just that. Maybe you want to see the player against better standard opposition than you have to date, or you give it six months and want to see how they have progressed, or 'kicked on' as we say. Generally, though, my view is that a thumbnail and a portrait should be enough from one scout to get a thorough opinion of a player into the system.

It is worth mentioning another different type of bias at this point. This is *age bias*. It is the fact that players born early on in an age group year are disproportionately represented in selection compared to the younger ones. In England our age groups start on 1 September each year; that is, they are based on the school year. Premier League footballers are much more likely to have been born in the first quarter of their age group year (i.e. September to November). The explanation usually given for this is that at the younger ages – from five years old upwards – the older ones in any age group often have a major physical advantage. They may well be the bigger and stronger and perhaps more physically literate youngsters, and as such they are more likely to be picked out. They then go on to get the training, the coaching and the game experience, which builds their advantage.

Internationally, UEFA and FIFA moved during 1995 to 1997 to a calendar year basis for age groups, starting from 1 January. This is why international age groups are on a calendar year basis yet we in England remain on a school year basis. In terms of age bias, however, it does not matter when the age group year starts. Over time the older ones still get the same advantage, except internationally it would be those born between January and March – the first quarter of their age group year. There is a huge amount of academic study around this phenomenon.[3]

You might say as a scout, 'Well, okay, that's tough on the younger ones but our job is to pick out the best players, so what does it matter to us?' The problem is, if we look further into the relative age-effect evidence, the bias tends to even itself out as the players get older. There is less of an evident age bias once they get to senior levels. The evidence, in fact, suggests that the younger ones who survive in the system do proportionately better at the very highest level than the older ones. This may be because they have had to battle against the age effect. Either way, it tells us as scouts that we need to be aware of age.

It seems clear that this age bias is a recruitment issue at heart. Once a player is in an academy, a good academy will consider their dates of birth and other significant factors, such as their relative physical maturity and emotional literacy ages. Players should

---

3 I would recommend 'Relative Age Effect' on www.playerdevelopment. com as a good summary.

have individual development plans that help balance their development, which may include such things as playing up or playing down in the ages and so forth. Most academies play some games based on calendar year groups (often in preparation for overseas tournaments) or have 'bio-banding' games linking players of different physical maturity together from time to time.

The only way to eradicate the age bias effect within an academy is to adopt 'birthday banding'. This is where an age group is based simply on the players' age. So your '10s' group will have all those aged ten. When a player gets to their 11th birthday they move up to the '11s' and so on. This is arguably the only system whereby every player will experience at some time over 12 months being the youngest and then the oldest in their age group. (I piloted just such a system at Chelsea academy in our trials programme and it worked well; however, we kept having to 'translate' players back to their conventional school year age group in the academy during our discussions when it came to assessing them or comparing them with existing signed players.)

Of course, we can argue that the relative age effect will operate from grassroots and school anyway, so an academy changing its age structure in isolation will have a limited effect. Particularly, as I have said, because a good academy will have an individual development plan for each player once signed.

However, that is enough about age here, just to say that a scout needs to be aware if they possibly can be of a player's date of birth to be able to assess them properly. We are not often told that when academy scouting, which means we need to cultivate other sources of information or intelligence.

Aside from performance assessment and the reports that follow from that, a scout will also usually be expected to be able to gather background information on a player, particularly if they begin to be of interest to a club. In grassroots scouting it is relatively easy to ask the player's club about his background (and date of birth) and you may well be able to legitimately be in touch with parents as well. However, in academy scouting and senior scouting you will be dealing with signed players, and you cannot make direct approaches to a player (of any age) who is signed on a contract or with an academy registration with another pro club.

In these circumstances, we need to use our networks. I will talk later about specific networks associated with each type of scouting, but it is enough here to mention that, when at games reporting on a player's performance in the game itself, you are looking for clues about their character. You might see glimpses of that in the warm-up – another very good reason to get to the game well in advance of kick-off – or in the player's interaction with coaches and team-mates. All this comes down to observation and concentration by the scout when covering a game. There is more than just the 90-plus minutes of football action to be covered.

Beyond this we are looking at gathering intelligence on a player from social media and from your contacts. There are issues with this, of course, depending on the age of the player. There are obvious safeguarding concerns about tracking minors through social media. For those over 18 years of age, Instagram, TikTok and other platforms can provide us with a lot of information. There is software available now that assesses a player's social media profile, such as their X (previously Twitter) feed. I know of one current England international who had interest from another Premier League club stalled because the club had noticed through their software that the words 'Nando's' and 'takeaways' seemed to come up a lot! This alerted the club to possible lifestyle issues with the player, who indeed has had weight issues from time to time.

There are other reasons to tread carefully with social media contacts. I was told by my boss at one stage that a u18 player at a local club was seeking a move. He had been told this by another agent – not the lad's agent. He asked me to get together our reports on the player and do some background digging. One of the things I did was to start following the lad on Instagram. Just a few hours later my boss was phoning me, saying, 'Chris, what are you doing? You're killing us! The player has been on to his agent all excited, saying, "Chris Robinson is following me on Instagram – are they interested in signing me?"' The lad's agent was straight on to my boss. So, tread carefully. There are other ways to get the research done. The simplest is to get someone else to do it for you!

Overall then, we need to report carefully and professionally on a player. These reports are our product. We will also need to gather a full picture of the player through our networks, contacts and research. This is all part of reporting on a player in a professional way.

Follow the QR code for a video of me talking about reporting:

Chapter Six

Grassroots Scouting

WHEN I was a kid aged about six or seven I remember my dad taking me over to Hackney Marshes for the first time. This was a Sunday morning. I can remember vividly standing in the middle of the mass of pitches, with football everywhere around me, as far as I could see. I believe there were over a hundred pitches. It was heaven for me. The standard of football varied hugely but was invariably entertaining. I loved it. The heart of the beautiful game.

We all start at the grassroots one way or another. Again looking back, when I was of school age there was very little club football at all. It was all centred around school football and then districts and counties up to England Schoolboys. If you read the biographies of the old stars – as I do – usually they were scouted in the 1940s and 50s at school or representative games.

It did vary around the country but that was the usual focus of schoolboy football.

Now, of course, it is the other way round. The norm is club football, and school football is hit-and-miss around the country. There is now a huge range of club football for kids aged 6 to 18. Some clubs run multiple teams of all ages. There are some issues here, though. Clubs usually have to pay out for pitch hire, refs and kit.

Sponsorships are hard to come by. Consequently, most local clubs charge parents 'subs' or match fees to cover the costs. That's inevitable, and many clubs work really hard to limit the costs to parents where they can. However, it does mean there may well be kids who do not access club football because their families cannot afford the costs, and we, as scouts, need to be aware of that.

There may be other reasons kids do not access club football. Families may not be supporting them for various reasons, so there may not be anyone to contact a club, get them to training or games or whatever. I read of one coach who said that when he was a young player he hardly got to play club football because where he grew up most of the leagues played Saturday mornings and he had to attend religious school on Saturday mornings.

We will discuss later the various other ways to access young players because of these and other considerations that may limit their involvement in mainstream club football. However, for now let's look at that mainstream and what it means to scout grassroots club football. By 'grassroots' I mean the football that happens in local parks and recreation grounds and on school pitches pretty much every weekend all over the country. This is where local heroes give up so much time to organise clubs, act as refs, put goals up and take them down again, mark out pitches and wash kits. This is the lifeblood of football in this country. And it is where nearly all players start off.

There will be local variation. In some areas clubs will not be involved in games against other clubs at the u6 age. In other areas there are thriving u6 leagues (although not usually recording results). Some leagues will play on Saturday mornings and some on Sundays – either morning or afternoon. So, if you are going to scout grassroots football diligently, you can expect to be out on Saturday mornings and most of Sundays. Are you ready for that?

So how do you start? Let's assume you are working for a club. You need to find out where the games are. I would always recommend that grassroots scouts be allocated to local geographical areas rather than on any other basis – an age-group focus, for example, across a region – because you need to build local knowledge, and the crucial element for a top grassroots scout is a network of contacts. It is much more feasible to do that in a defined geographical area.

Given this local focus, you may already know where there are a lot of games played at the weekends in your area – the local park, recreation ground, school fields, etc. This is your starting point. It is, of course, much more time-efficient to go where you can watch several games over a couple of hours. It is a numbers game to some extent. You need to watch a lot of players.

As you build your network – and we will come to how to do that – you will be tipped off about players, or if you want to follow up on players at certain target ages, you will need to find out what the fixtures are. League websites are the obvious first port of call. They vary hugely in their efficiency and accessibility. Some will list updated fixtures with kick-off times and venues. Some will even have squad lists, top scorers and so on. However, some may deny access unless you have a log-on from a club.

Similarly, club websites vary too, although a lot of clubs use Facebook or other social media rather than updating websites. It is all a matter of research. Get your laptop out or get on a PC or even your phone and go searching for that info. As your network builds it will be easier to get information on who is playing well.

Your club may well – and really should, in fact – let you know priority ages and positions that they are looking for. You might match up those target ages and key fixtures, and off you go. It does, naturally, make sense to start with the best divisions in the best leagues and work down. There are many cases of good young players playing in relatively low-standard leagues because they like to play with their mates or whatever. However, from a time efficiency point of view, it makes sense to assume by and large that the better teams have the better players.

You might in practice combine this targeted approach with the opportunity to look around. For example, some years ago when I was doing grassroots scouting I went to watch a game down at Angmering in West Sussex because I knew a player I had seen previously was playing there. I watched his game – at u12s – and having spoken to the manager and parents of the target player, I watched the last ten minutes of a u15 game on the next pitch. There was a well-built left-footed centre-back playing in the u15 game, and he did well. He was athletic and mobile and was an effective defender, although maybe not a great player technically. I spoke to his team coach, who as it turned out was his dad (the coach is often the dad of the best player at the grassroots level!), and noted some information. This player was not at our standard, but he was useful. I passed his info on to our local college programme.

A while later I heard he was in our college programme and doing well. I watched him again there just to check his level. He was still not for us, but progressing. Later still I heard that he had received a scholarship to go to an American college to play football and is there now, which is no doubt a life-changing experience for him. I do not know whether he ever knew of my little part in his journey, but it was a chance thing, and all because I bothered to watch the game on the next pitch to the one I was really there for – and had a good network.

Okay, you are at a game at the target age and you see a player you like, and he is in a priority position. What do you do? The ideal is that you will need to see him again – another day, another game.

If you are there in advance of the game, then at a suitable point – not when the coach is in the middle of a warm-up – you should introduce yourself to the coach just to let them know you are there. I would normally say something like, 'Hi, I'm Chris Robinson from xxxxx club, here to watch the game. Look, I know you are busy now, but we can have a chat after the game. I'll leave you to it … good luck.' At the end of the game, I would approach the coach again even if I did not have a specific player to follow up with. I would not do this during the game – you must respect they are busy then. They will usually have a few words with their team after the final whistle and you want to respect that too, but you do not want to wait too long because you do not want the parents to have gone either.

The key point here, if you have a player of interest, is that in the first instance you approach the coach, not the parent. This is important. You must respect the conventions and requirements of the game. (Most clubs have developed their own code of conduct for scouts, but as an example see the Professional Football Scouts Association (PFSA) Scout Code of Conduct in Appendix 1.)

Another key point here is that I would invariably be in club kit. Some clubs do not provide scouts with kit, so for some it may just be a coat. Some scouts prefer to be incognito. My view on this is clear. The ideal is for the scout to wear club kit. We want them to look professional. We want players, club officials and parents to know that as a professional club we are interested in their games, their players and their leagues. Wearing club kit is also a matter of good practice in terms of safeguarding. We should make it clear who we are and who we represent.

I would then show the coach my club identification. This is mandatory – again from a safeguarding point of view. You must have an up-to-date club badge with a photo, properly authorised, identifying you as a scout. This is not optional, it is mandatory, and all reputable clubs know this and abide by the requirements.

Also, in my view, it is professional and sensible to have a business card to give out in these circumstances.[4] The bigger clubs will provide these to scouts as a matter of course, but I do realise that perhaps not all clubs have the resources to do this. However, it is very helpful. So I would then give the coach one of my cards and say we can chat after the game, or if I have arrived during the game and have not spoken to them before, I would continue: 'Well done today,' or 'Hard luck today,' or whatever suits the occasion, then 'I liked your number x. What can you tell me about them?'

Then you are off and running. Your objective might be at this stage to find out a bit more about the

---

4   A lot of clubs are now moving to digital cards.

player with the idea that you will be watching him again. If you want to bring him in to a trial or filter event, then you will need to speak to his parents. You need the coach to point them out to you or ideally introduce you to them. The coach may offer to introduce you to the parents anyway, which is fine.

If you do not have a specific player to follow up on, this is a great opportunity to build your network anyway. Most coaches are only too happy to chat about their league or their season so far, so I might say, 'How's your season going? I see you're third in the league?' Then at some point, I have two key questions: 'Who is the best team you have played this season?' and 'Who is the best player you've played against this season?'

All this info – including the coach's name and mobile number – and any details from parents on a player, you are recording in your notebook or on your phone, whichever suits you. This is your bread and butter of scouting.

When talking to parents you need to be clear about what your objective is. If you want to bring the player into a trial or event, then you need the details of that and to tell them you will follow up by email with those details from the club. If you are just gathering info and want to see the player again, then tell them that is what you intend to do. I always try to talk to parents away from other parents if I can, but you sometimes have to take things as they are when pitchside.

These conversations and approaches are what have worked well for me. You will find your way to make these connections. The point here is that you have a couple of key objectives to be met:

1. Getting info as needed on specific players, including parent details.

2. Building your network.

Most coaches and most parents in my experience are flattered that a professional club is interested in them, so they are receptive and positive. A professional and personable approach from the scout increases the chances of that happening.

Occasionally you will get knocked back. There are coaches who for one reason or another will not want their players to go to a pro club – or not your clubs anyway. They may be linked to another club themselves. They may have had a bad experience with an academy somewhere along the line – perhaps with one of their own children or even themselves.

When I worked at Portsmouth FC I did on a couple of occasions come across diehard Southampton fans who were not keen, but to be fair, even in those circumstances, they did not stop players going into a rival club.

On rare occasions, club coaches will work to prevent players from coming into academies, as I say. I recall one good club team in Surrey where the coach resisted his key players coming into academies over a few seasons. They were winning everything locally and that was obviously the coach's priority. I did also hear he'd had a bad experience at an academy with his own son – who was one of the players in his team, although not one of the best ones – some years previously.

I might note here in passing that a 'bad experience' for some parents might just mean their son was not signed. There are various books out there that seem at heart to be a rant against academies, and the main source of that seems to be that players get rejected. I am not in any way excusing bad practices among academies in the way trialists are treated and dealt with. No one likes to hear of the heartache that can be involved and the way this affects some young players. We can all improve on the trial processes and many clubs are trying hard to do just that. I will talk about trials later. However, I will say here that this is an elite sport. That means selection, and therefore rejection too – usually for most of the players involved. However carefully and sensitively it is done – and many clubs do it very well – that word 'no' sticks with some parents and some players too.

Anyway, back to that Surrey-based team. The coach's usual response to enquiries from academy scouts was that there was plenty of time, and maybe when they were older they could come back. I did say to the coach that some of these players would miss the boat. A player who is at academy level at 12 years of age will usually fall behind the level by age 14 or 15 because of the better coaching and games programme in a good academy. It becomes harder and harder for players to jump across from grassroots to academy football from 13 onwards – particularly where Category 1 academies are concerned.

I did get that team's best player – a forward – in for a trial game eventually at u16 last season and he was way off the standard by then – yet at u12 I think we would have signed him. That is a great shame.

I must stress that this resistance is rare, and the great majority of coaches want their players to succeed and progress and are helpful to and cooperative with scouts. But if you as a scout do get a knockback from a club coach, you need to think of another route to the player, particularly if you have reason to believe the parents of that player have not been given the choice themselves. You will need to do some digging and find out whether the player plays for his school or maybe district, or even another club on a different day, and then repeat the process through that channel.

Building a network is the key to successful grassroots scouting. One of the most experienced and successful scouts at Chelsea is Ray Rembridge, who had over 60 players signed by the academy, including talent such as Reece James, Trevoh Chalobah and Conor Gallagher. I have been to many grounds and venues with Ray over the years and learned a lot from him. One thing that struck me early on was that if I went to a grassroots venue or tournament with Ray, or a non-league ground to watch youth games, it would take an age to walk to the pitch we were aiming for. This is because so many people would stop him to say hello and have a chat – every five metres or so along a touchline there would be someone else! There are two significant factors here. The first is that Ray has worked in the same area for a long time and has built up many contacts.

The second is that most of these people would describe Ray in the same way – as a 'gentleman'. That is the most common word used to describe him. So people know him, and they trust him. Add that to the fact that he has a great eye for talent and knows the game well at all levels, then you have the ingredients of a really top scout.

There are other ways to build your network. Many academies will hold 'coaches' evenings' where they get local coaches in from grassroots clubs and show them around their training ground, give them some presentations on how their academy works and what they are looking for and usually let them watch training or even share some coaching resources. These evenings – they usually are evenings – are easy to organise and cost virtually nothing, yet they are much valued by local coaches. We did them for years at Chelsea, and when I worked in grassroots scouting I organised many such events every season. Many clubs do the same or similar. I recommend them to you as ways to build networks.

The key priority recruitment age for many top clubs now is six and seven years of age. You cannot sign for an academy until you are approaching your u9 season, but all academies run 'pre-academy' programmes of one sort or another, usually featuring pre-academy 'development centres'. Thus, the competition for those top u8s is fierce in many areas. This is because most clubs understand that if you can get the very best talent in at u9 you have a great base to start from. These players will be with you the longest, and if they progress they grow up with you.

A lot of top academies' recruitment strategies have been built around getting the very best talent you can at u9. This means you do not need to sign so many at other ages where the jump across from grassroots to an academy gets harder and harder, as I have said. So at Chelsea, for example, many of the top talents now playing first-team football at the club or elsewhere – Mason Mount, Ruben Loftus-Cheek, Callum Hudson-Odoi, Reece James, Conor Gallagher and so on – signed at u9 and had often been at the club since age six or seven.

Academies usually sign about 16 to 20 u9s each season, whereas from u9 up to u16 they may not sign that many from grassroots across all the ages combined in any one season. So if you as a scout want to work in the very top priority recruitment ages and want to get lots of players signed, then pre-academy is the focus for you. The age ranges of six and seven bring their specialist requirements and networks. I must say I have never really focused on those early ages myself, although I did run a development centre for Portsmouth as coach and scout at one stage and have had players signed at u9. It is quite a specialist area, in my view, to be able to identify talent in such young players but an essential one for any academy and top scouts such as Ray Rembridge and Sean Conlon at Chelsea, for example, who are very good at identifying and recruiting these youngsters.

Another key aspect of grassroots scouting for all ages is tournaments. These are usually in summer, although not exclusively. For many local clubs they represent a major money-spinner. Clubs pay to enter tournaments and spectators may pay for parking, programmes and so on. This is now a key part of the grassroots clubs' economy. However, it does bring a bit of a problem in that, certainly pre-Covid, every club seemed to want to run their own tournament and you could turn up for some and there would be hardly any clubs there, and every age group was filled with teams mostly from the host club themselves. You will need to be selective. More recently some clubs have sadly struggled to organise these tournaments because of a lack of volunteers, and that is a great shame. I often enjoyed the summer tournaments. Although I did not really do grassroots scouting any more, I volunteered to go to one near me last summer to help our local scouting team. There is usually good weather, as they are mostly in summer, and it can be a very pleasant day with families enjoying themselves and a lot of fun football on show.

The local county FAs will usually list the tournaments they have sanctioned so they can be a good guide to what's on. Some tournaments attract teams from all over and can be of a very good standard. Many are held over a weekend with the age groups split over the two days – so if you are interested in one or two ages you need to look on the club website and see which age group is playing when. Some of the club websites will give you a running order that lists the clubs involved and you can get a good feel for the size and standard of the tournament from that.

It is good practice when you arrive at a tournament to find the organisers' control point to let them know you are there, showing your club badge. It is just a matter of courtesy really, but the organisers usually appreciate it.

Some tournaments are big. The one I went to last summer at Worthing United was huge. In my area, the Petersfield Town tournament is also known as a good one with a lot of clubs coming into it. I have found that it is better at these big tournaments if you focus on one target age group. Otherwise, you can wander round and see a mass of football but not really get the lie of the land and scout anything thoroughly. It is not unusual for the big academies to have two or three scouts at the big tournaments.

While school football has indeed declined in terms of significance, it still happens and can still be a source of good games to scout. Again, local knowledge is the key – which schools have good teams, which encourage football? Contact with PE teachers – especially those who may coordinate games between local schools – is very helpful and a key part of your network. The schools more interested in football will enter the English Schools Football Association (ESFA) cups, which are significant competitions. There are various age groups and categories of schools, but the ESFA website will show you the fixtures. The finals are usually at a pro ground and are often featured live on YouTube.

In some parts of the country, district and county football is important and well organised, but in others it is less so, and sometimes virtually non-existent. The district teams may well start at u11 and go up from there. In Hampshire there is a regular league of district teams playing their games on Saturday mornings. It is once again a case of doing your research online and asking your growing network where there is district football. It is the same with county football – the county FAs may have some links on their sites and there may be county school FAs too. As with local clubs, many are now using Facebook and other social media channels rather than websites.

The people running district and county representative teams – and those running league rep teams where they exist – are key people to cultivate as they will be familiar with a range of players across different schools or clubs. Signed academy players may also play in district or county teams so it is an opportunity to watch them away from their clubs, but their presence can help give you a standard to judge other players by too.

The rise of 'showcase' teams has been a feature of the grassroots landscape over the last ten years. There are now dozens of these organisations in each region. They exist to provide a platform for players to show their talents to pro clubs. They are often focused on the u15–u16 age groups, aiming to get players picked up for scholarships at pro clubs. Players will often pay to be featured in these games.

The bigger and better-established organisations, such as Rising Ballers, Pro-Direct, Kinetic and Pulse, have thrived and offer a range of coaching and playing opportunities, perhaps branching off into college schemes or feeding senior teams. They are often well organised and well coached. It is, however, difficult to keep up with the range of other showcase organisations popping up all over, particularly in the urban areas. It is not unusual for some players to be playing for a handful of different organisations or moving about from one to the other. Nevertheless, they do work as a platform for talent, and as a scout you need to know who they are and get to watch them if they cover your age groups. Many of the pro academies will regularly invite these showcase organisations into their training grounds for games. They are an important part of the local football scene now, particularly in London.

In a similar way, 'soccer schools' have been a part of the grassroots scene for many years. These will often operate right across the age ranges from u6 up and offer training on one or two nights a week. The players will usually play for various clubs at the weekend, but the soccer schools offer a good opportunity to watch talent on midweek nights and are an important part of your network as a scout. Some, such as the Elite Training Centre in the Southampton-Portsmouth area and All-Stars at Eastbourne, have a tradition of developing players who go into academies and operate at a high standard of coaching and facilities.

Your club may have a community or foundation arm. This type of activity – which used to come under the banner of 'Football in the Community' – can be extensive. The Chelsea FC Foundation is probably the largest in the world, working with over a million children a year around the globe, and when I was there we worked hard to establish progression pathways for players and coaches from the foundation into the academy, with a lot of success. However, at a lot of clubs, although the community work may not be on the same scale as Chelsea, they are often overlooked by scouts, and this is a mistake. The coaches at the community activities may well be active in football in the area in other ways – with local clubs or whatever – so again provide a networking opportunity.

The foundations or community arms are not always organised in the same way. For some years the 'Arsenal Soccer School' was a franchise operation. The excellent Manchester United Foundation was more of a separate arm of the club. It is quite rare, as at Chelsea, for the foundation to be an integral part of the structure of the mainstream club.

One limiting factor of soccer schools, some showcase organisations and some club community activity is that it is 'pay for play' – there is a cost to the players. This still means they are worth scouting – as we have seen, local grassroots club football comes at a cost too. However, we need to remember, as scouts, that there will be some kids who cannot get into those shop windows for lack of money. School football is still important in this respect, therefore, as it is free, but as noted it is patchy and not as widespread or common as it used to be. As scouts you are going to have to go one step further and be proactive, as many clubs are.

You can organise talent ID events yourself and aim at the geographical area and age group you want to target. You pick an area and an age group and find a central venue – maybe a five-a-side centre or one of the local schools may help. Pick a time that will work for that age group; if you are aiming at u6s you do not want the event going on past 7pm. You then contact all the local schools – by email, phone or letter – and ask them to send their best three players at that age to the event, and they do that by contacting you for details (otherwise you will not know how many kids are coming). Some schools will ignore the contact, some will help. Your network comes into play, and if you stick at it you will build these events over time. You organise coaches and equipment and then have yourself a local talent ID event.

The joy of this is that kids do not have to pay or travel far to get to the event. One such event we organised in south London some years ago had a little lad turn up in jeans – he had no football kit. He is now playing Premier League football.

I want to specifically mention girls' football. For years, of course, scouts have been used to seeing some girls playing in the younger ages with the boys up until around u12. However, scouts often did not know where to signpost girls that they saw who looked good players. With the growth and development of girls' football there does seem to be fewer girls playing in boys teams now as they have more options in girls-only football.

There are challenges with girls' football, and comments in response to our 'The Scouting Game' social media videos and posts have highlighted some of these. A lot of what I say in this book about what scouts look for, ideal positional profiles and how to assess and report on players, applies equally to girls and boys, women and men. It must be said, though, that the structures they can be scouted into are not the same. There are very few scouts employed to focus on the girls' game. Most major clubs still seem to rely on open trials, often held in summer. As we mention elsewhere in this book, open trial days are still used and have been productive to an extent in the game over the years, but to my mind they are hit-and-miss affairs. They will not suit every player; many will not stand out in brief viewings or might have an off day or whatever. They can still be useful but only as an addition to proper conventional scouting where professional scouts go out and unearth talent.

There was a recent article in *The Athletic*, the online football news magazine, which also picked up on this issue:

> Having won the Division 1 Feminine a record 16 times and with eight Women's Champions League (UWCL) titles to their name, it might come as a surprise to learn that Lyon do not have any scouts.
>
> They're not alone. Neither do two-time UWCL winners Wolfsburg. In fact, most Women's Super League (WSL) clubs, including Manchester United, do not have such roles.
>
> This is in stark contrast to some Premier League clubs who can tap into extensive networks of anything up to 50 international scouts. Newcastle United, for example, have recently recruited six scouts for South America, while Everton have dedicated recruitment leads in France, Spain and Portugal. In contrast, scouts are a rare breed in women's football.[5]

The article goes on to look at the increasing role that data is playing in recruitment in the women's game,

---

5   *The Athletic*, 2 January 2024.

as it does in the men's. However, while some clubs are building their scouting resources in the girls' and women's game, the point is well made that they have a long way to go.

Surely the girls' and women's games have evolved enough now to be able to deliver widespread effective scouting at the grassroots level? There must be enough girls' football to make that viable now. It seems to me that talent must be being missed and that is always a worry to me as a scout in any context. It is up to the major clubs involved to ensure that, if they want the girls' and women's game to continue to develop and grow, they invest in proper talent identification systems. Perhaps it is happening and will take time but the feedback I have had from parents seems to suggest there is talent out there crying out to be found.

Back to the broader view of football, there are other specific initiatives that you as a scout can arrange to reach out to talent in different ways. You can have targeted events such as 'goalie wars', 'street football' (open three-a-side tournaments) or 'striker clinics' – again depending on what your priorities are. With a little imagination and organisation, and at relatively low cost, you can find other ways to locate talent that does not come through the mainstream club or soccer school channels.

You might like to target certain communities where you feel you are not making much headway through conventional means. For example, in certain parts of London, the Pakistani and Bangladeshi communities are significant. They can be third or fourth generation UK citizens and have grown up in a football culture. However, very few kids from these communities are breaking through into professional academies and on to professional football. We look at this issue in more detail in Chapter Twelve.

Chelsea ran the 'Asian Star' programme over many years and held specific events with the Polish and Somalian communities, among others, to good effect. My point here is that as a scout you need to think smart and that will take you to a lot of local league games and rec grounds and a lot of sunny summer tournaments, but also to schools and showcase events and to meet the range of communities that will be there in your area. You will need to be ready to create open-access events if you are really going to do the job right!

Grassroots scouting can be seen as wandering along to your local park and watching a couple of games. That may work for you and your club. I have found you need to do a lot more to succeed as a top grassroots scout. You need to build a network, do a lot of research, think about the area you are in and where all the talent might be – and then reach out for it.

See my video on how to get a trial:

Chapter Seven

Academy Scouting

WHEN I arrived at the training ground I was told there was nowhere to park. The burly steward, unshaven and jowly, in a high-viz once-yellow jacket, waved me away contemptuously.

'You'll have to park on the street somewhere. No parking here for scouts.'

I eventually found somewhere to park and hiked back in the drizzling rain of a cold November Sunday morning in the London suburbs, which looked grey and uninviting. I told the grumpy steward my name, what club I was from and that I'd had email permission to attend their academy ground that morning to watch a u13 game.

'What email?' he asked suspiciously.

I dug out my phone from under my long raincoat and showed him. He squinted at the phone, then grunted and said, 'You'll have to wait there till near kick-off time.' He nodded towards the side of the gate where another forlorn figure stood in the rain. He peered at me from under a blank cap, which had water dripping off the peak. I walked over.

'Scout?' he asked.

I said I was and introduced myself. We shook damp hands. He was from a Midlands club, and I had never met him before.

'Is it always like this here?' he asked from the side of his mouth as we stood shivering by the hedge.

'Like what?'

'So bloody unfriendly.' He nodded towards the steward.

'Oh, right. Yes, you've seen nothing yet,' I muttered.

We could see far across the training ground that the teams of various ages on various pitches were out and warming up. I went back to the steward. 'We're going to miss the kick-off if we have to wait much longer!' I said to him. He shrugged.

'You won't miss much.'

I was not sure whether he was referring to the expected timescale or the quality of the teams we were there to watch. His walkie-talkie attached to his collar squawked and he pressed it. There was a mixture of static and a garbled voice at the other end, so I could only hear his end of the conversation.

'Yeah … yeah … right … well, two of 'em. Under 13s … both … okay.' He sighed heavily as if he had the world on his scruffy viz-clad shoulders. 'Come on then.' Clearly he was doing us some huge favour. He set off – but not towards the matches that were kicking off in the far distance.

I called after him, 'Isn't that the under-13 game over there?'

'I've got to take you round the outside,' he said, as if it was so obvious. I looked at the other scout. We both looked across the empty space to the far games and then at the steward, who was shuffling slowly round the perimeter of the training ground away to our right. 'Come on, then,' he called over his shoulder.

We followed him. We walked right around the far edge of the training ground and finally got to the u13 game we were both there to watch. It was about ten minutes in by the time we got to the pitch.

'Laughing Boy', the steward, took us to a place near a far corner flag where there was a small five-metre box of cones set out, set some five metres back from the pitch up against a rough, uneven wire fence, among overgrown scrubby grass. A bedraggled swaybacked grey horse stood in the rain on the other side of the fence watching us balefully, almost pityingly.

'Stand in there,' he said.

The Midlands scout and I stood inside the cones. There was barely enough room for us to both stand up next to each other. The steward stood a couple of metres away, ever vigilant.

The drizzling rain continued. The game was as dismal as the weather. At half-time I felt the pre-match coffee I'd had was having its effect. I needed to go to the toilet. I turned to the steward. 'I need the gents,' I said. 'It's by the dressing rooms, isn't it?'

He looked from me to the other scout. 'You going too?' he asked the other guy.

'No, thanks,' he said.

The steward puzzled over this then turned away, talking into his walkie-talkie. I was not waiting. I set off towards the dressing rooms.

I could hear the steward talking more urgently into his walkie-talkie, almost hysterical. Ahead of me I could see another steward scuttling across the damp green of the training ground towards us. As we passed I heard the first, older, scout say, 'He's going to the toilets! You stay with him.' The second steward, a slim younger guy, also clad in a bulky, misshapen heavy jacket and high-viz, turned and walked alongside me.

The older steward turned hastily back to the bemused Midlands scout.

When we got to the old portacabin that was the toilets I turned and looked at the steward. 'You are coming inside with me?' I asked.

'Ah … no, no.' At least he had the grace to be shamefaced.

I was escorted back to our little cage of cones, and we watched the dreary second half then were escorted back right around the edge of the training ground and out of the gate.

The other scout and I paused briefly outside the gate. 'Well,' he said, 'that was fun.' We shook hands and went our separate ways.

At no time were we welcomed or offered tea or coffee or even any shelter. We were clearly not going to be given any team sheets, of course. We missed the start of the game because they kept us outside waiting and then walked us a ridiculously long way round. They clearly did not want us there and made it as difficult and unpleasant as possible. This was not an isolated case of poor practice or a mistake. It was a clear conscious policy on behalf of the host club.

This can be the reality of academy scouting. All I have set out here actually happened. However, I must say that not all academies are like that. Not by any means. At Chelsea, I am proud to say, given you have the right email permission and thus are on the security list, you are welcomed to the ground. You can go from match to match and stand or sit where you like – even among the parents – and there are a couple of catering vans where you can get a hot drink or food.

Why does this happen, though? Why are scouts watching other academies? And why are there these issues? Does it have to be a problem?

A few years ago I went to a tournament in the Netherlands that our u12s were playing in. I went to watch the opposition teams who were from some of the best clubs across Europe. At the entrance I was handed a complete list of all the teams competing, with squads' names set out with their dates of birth. I was directed to an upstairs lounge where there was complimentary coffee and pastries. I got talking there to the woman who oversaw the lounge. She pointed out that all the teams would play at some time on the pitch that the lounge overlooked. 'You can actually stay up here all day and see everything from a seat in the window!'

So I did. I sat on a barstool by the ledge that ran along the windows so I could write my notes easily, with my squad lists laid out alongside me. The hospitable staff kept me fed and watered, bringing me hot drinks and food all day. A couple of times during the day one of the organising club's officials came up to check I was okay and had everything I needed, and on each occasion we sat and talked football for a while.

In 2012 the Premier League introduced the 'Elite Player Performance Plan' (EPPP), as mentioned before. This was a major step forward for football youth development in this country. It reorganised and greatly improved the professionalism of our youth game. It set up the framework that academies now work under, although it has been revised and updated virtually every year.

Before the EPPP, the set-up of academies – or 'centres of excellence' as most of them were previously called – was haphazard. This affected scouting at them too. You could just turn up at a venue, and if you were questioned by a steward (if there was one) you could just say, 'I've come to watch my nephew play,' and they would wave you in. I did sometimes think that if all the stewards in clubs across London got together and compared notes they would have concluded I had a huge family!

Two of the major changes that the EPPP introduced were that an academy could now formally get a representative in to watch a game if they emailed 48 hours in advance and the representative had suitable identification, and also the idea of compensation for academy players was formally codified. I will discuss both aspects later in more detail, but this was a game-changing moment. It will come as a surprise to many people – including many parents – that clubs can 'buy' a player aged from 9 to 18 years of age from another club. As we will see, it is not quite as simple as that, but in principle it is there.

These developments were not popular with all clubs. Some of the smaller clubs felt this scouting access and compensation system would just open the door for the big clubs to come swooping in and steal away their best talent. To some extent, this was the idea, to be fair, given the notion of 'the best with the best' that underpinned the EPPP. However, the smaller clubs also complained that the compensation scheme was not generous enough. Beyond that, some smaller clubs felt the increased costs of better-staffed and structured academies were beyond them, despite the financial help that came along with the plan.

Nevertheless, the plan established the formal acknowledgement that a club could send a scout to watch another academy and ultimately there was a process set out for a young player to change from one academy to another. Consequently, from 2012 onwards, clubs have largely upgraded their academy scouting programmes.

Again, it varies from one club to another. The larger clubs will usually have a team of scouts who are focused on scouting at other academies. They will have recruitment analysts in the major clubs working with this academy scouting team. They will log their work through systems such as Scout7 or Wyscout, or have their own in-house database systems. It has become quite a sophisticated operation at the highest level. The smaller clubs may only have one or two scouts, if that, who cover academy football. Given that you do not get team sheets other than at the higher levels of u18, the identification of players is a real challenge and this restricts data gathering and analysis. We will come back to the issues caused by this dearth of information later.

The big academies will have a strong team within their hour-and-a-half local catchment area, but also 'national' scouts spread around the other urban areas. So, for example, the bigger northern clubs such as Manchester City, Manchester United and Liverpool all have scouts covering London, usually from the u13 age upwards.

Generally the bigger clubs are looking for players to sign. However, there is also the issue of players who may be released from a club – other academies will need to know who those players are to decide whether they want to sign them. So scouts are needed to identify players of interest.

The EPPP set up a system of four levels of academy. 'Category 1' is the top standard, with a minimum staffing requirement and standard of facilities. Then there is 'Category 2' and 'Category 3', each with slightly fewer requirements in terms of staffing and facilities. 'Category 4' covers the clubs who just run a u18 set-up and not a full academy. Clubs are reassessed and audited at least every two years and can move up or down the system as a result.

So if you go to an academy game – at any age group – you might see a scout or two, often in a 'box' of cones in a corner, watching. They are usually kept away from parents. In fact, the Premier League code of conduct makes it clear that scouts must not directly approach parents of players signed to other clubs. Many academies have responded by deciding that scouts need to be isolated like the 'great unwashed' and kept as far from parents as possible. A few – as we have learned – take that to extremes and make scouts feel decidedly unwelcome. A few treat scouts like adults and then expect them to behave properly, but sadly this is the exception rather than anywhere near the rule.

How does it work in practice then? As a scout, the first thing is to find out the fixtures. Your coordinator at your club will probably do this and allocate games to you. The formal fixtures come out via the Premier League for Category 1 and 2 academies, and the Football League for the Category 3 clubs. This basic programme follows a regular pattern.

The u16s and u18s mostly play on Saturday mornings. Usually, the fixtures will only show the u18s games and you have to assume the u16s will play at the same time and place. The u9 to u15s play on Sundays. The fixture list will just show the clubs – for example, 'Chelsea v Arsenal' – so you have to assume that the 'evens', the u10s, u12s and u14s will play at Chelsea and the 'odds', the u9s, u11s, u13s and u15s, will play at Arsenal. However, frustratingly, it does not always follow this pattern and it is not until you hear back from the club you request permission from that you find out for sure who is where. Of course, if you are smart and have built a good network of contacts, you can find out through other means.

You – or your club coordinator or recruitment administrator (whoever organises and schedules scout attendance at academy games in your club) – will send an email to the host club asking permission for their named scout to attend. This must be done no later than 12 noon on the last working day before the game (it used to be 48 hours before the kick-off). The host club should then email back to your club – usually the day before the game – giving permission and confirming the kick-off time and venue. However, if you have asked for a u11 game and the club has decided the u11s will be playing away that week, then some clubs will reply just saying 'no such game'. Very unhelpful. Others may reply, 'No u11s game but the u10s and u12s are at home.'

Once you get your permission email back, you are set to attend. There is another 'however' here though! A lot of clubs are not well organised in their scouting permissions and must be chased up on the Friday, for example, before a Saturday game to give you a response. This is very frustrating because if the game is not on or you are denied permission for some reason, it is too late, in theory, to apply for another game elsewhere. This has led to scouts applying for various games to see which ones come back with permission.

This all only applies to games within the formal programme. There are no leagues as such from u9–u15, just these formal games programmes organised by the Premier League or the Football League. However, if you do get a fixture list, you will see there are a lot of gaps. Often, for example, there will be hardly any games listed between Christmas and the end of January. Partly this is to allow for the Christmas and New Year break, but also perhaps for any bad weather cancellations. Yet there will usually be games once the academies resume training in early January.

So at these times – and for other gaps or free weekends throughout the season – the academies will arrange games themselves. As these do not come under the banner of the formal programme, some academies will take that opportunity to deny scouts access, as 'they are not part of the formal programme'. This is all a nonsense, of course, but it happens very regularly. It is just an excuse for those clubs who do not want scouts to attend to deny permission, and the Premier League allows them to get away with it. The significant step that was taken by the Premier League in the EPPP, that of formally recognising the role and legitimacy of scouts attending matches, is undermined by them turning a blind eye to some academies denying access whenever they can get away with it.

What is it these clubs are afraid of? Presumably, it is scouts talking directly to the families of signed players and 'tapping them up' to leave and come and sign for them. Firstly, the point is that these are almost all signed players. They cannot just up and leave, even if they want to. We will talk more about registrations and players leaving one academy to join another later in this chapter. The point here is that, presumably, this is what those anxious academies are afraid of. In fact, some of the more confident clubs that let scouts come in and go where they want, take the view that admission to the game is not an issue, but the scouts' behaviour can be. So scouts can go where they like, but if they approach players' families this is the issue to be dealt with as it is clearly against the Premier League code of conduct for scouts. This can then be dealt with appropriately.

In this way, the more confident academies treat scouts as responsible professionals – unless and until they are given cause to doubt that. This seems to me a much more mature and balanced approach than those academies that refuse scouts entry whenever they can get away with doing so, or they treat scouts like scum when they do come in, as described at the beginning of the chapter.

Actually, I do not understand why scouts need permission at all to attend games. As long as a scout has an up-to-date valid pass with photograph from their club, which we all need to have anyway, then in my opinion they should be able to attend any academy match at any ground. Why not? It would cut down on a lot of work and emails, for sure. Scouts could still check which games are actually on and where if they need to, but it would just cut out some awkward unnecessary bureaucracy and poor practice in one fell swoop. It is not as if academies are going to be deluged with unmanageable numbers of scouts.

When you do get to games you will not be told the names of the players involved unless it is a Category 1 or 2 u18 game. In practice, scouts and teams of scouts build up knowledge of who is playing where and, as we shall hear, some share that knowledge. As I made clear earlier, this is not the case in many other countries in Europe where team sheets, often including dates of birth, are made available.

As it is, in this country, once a scout gets permission to attend, they will not be told formally who they are watching. This is crazy, and again, in my view, unprofessional and disrespectful. Some academies when challenged plead that it is about safeguarding and protecting children by not giving out their names. I must say I think this is evasive. For Premier League Cup competitions, teams must show the Premier League passes of all their players to the opposition if required. By sharing team sheets with registered and safeguard-checked representatives of other clubs, I cannot see how that is a safeguarding issue. Again, in practice, I think it is more about this begrudging attitude towards scouts and scouting that still persists in many academies – even though their own scouts will suffer similar treatment when they are out on their behalf.

Setting the issue of the weekly team sheets aside, each academy will have a spreadsheet of signed players across all their age groups, often showing dates of birth too. These are updated a few times during the season as players are signed or released. Why do academies not circulate these lists of signed players among themselves on a regular basis? This would give scouts a good idea of who at least was in the age group squad they were going to watch, and by catching first names being called out during the game they could easily work out who is who. They can then focus on the real job – reporting on the players. Instead, scouts will spend most of the time trying to catch some names of the players involved and having half a picture at best. 'Their number eight was good. Slim, white lad, left-footed, moved very well. Called Sol or Saul or something.' It is so amateurish and demeaning.

At a scouts' course I suggested this to the assembled group of scouts from different clubs as we were all moaning about this lack of team sheets. 'I tell you what, guys,' I said, 'if we wait for the Premier League to sort this out or for clubs to agree collectively, we will wait a long time. I'm sure we all have lists of signed players across all our age groups. I'll swap ours with anyone else who gives me theirs.'

There were no takers. There was some sheepish muttering about 'my boss wouldn't agree' but no one took the step. So, to be fair, it is maybe not just the Premier League or the academies that need to be braver and clearer, maybe it is also us scouts and our recruitment teams that need to show some principles too. I must again stress that these are just my personal opinions and observations.

Another irony is that a lot of the updated and comprehensive information that we seek – about fixtures in and out of the programme, for example – is available to all clubs via the Premier League's own intranet system that all academies have access to and where each player's minutes are logged and so forth. Yet, as I understand it, the academies are told not to share this 'for recruitment purposes'. We do not need to invent any new technology or systems for better information sharing. They are already there and in daily use. It is just that we scouts are not considered worthy or professional enough to access the system directly.

So let's get back to the game. You have got into the ground and have been told where the age group you are there to watch are playing – or you are being escorted there by a steward. You might be in with the parents or left to stand where you like around the pitch or taken to a 'box of cones' that is the scouts' area, or 'cage' as many scouts will refer to it. There may be a couple of other scouts there or you may be on your own. For u18 or u21 games, or the floodlit ones, you might get the luxury of sitting in a stand under some shelter. Most times for general academy scouting you can expect to be out in the elements. You will learn to juggle an umbrella as the wind drives the rain across the open training ground, as well as your notebook, pen and maybe your phone, where the informal squad list might be! There might be somewhere where you can get a hot drink, although more often there is not! You will learn where the local cafes are that will be open on Saturday or Sunday mornings.

You might have developed your own information system as a scout, or your recruitment team may have a joint resource, so you have some idea of the names of players involved. You may be going to have a general scan of one or both teams – using the 'thumbnails' described in Chapter Five, for example – or looking at one player of interest, intending to compile a 'portrait' report on him.

At u9 and u10, the games are likely to be 7v7, and most academies will field two seven-a-side teams so you will potentially have a lot of players to scan. At u11 and u12 the games will normally be 9v9, and again there may be two teams per academy. Towards the end of the season the u12s may start to play a few 11v11 games. From u13 upwards it is 11v11.

Having said that, clubs will jointly agree to vary any of this as suits. It might be at u9 that one club likes a 5v5 format or that one club may not have many players available for whatever reason, or whatever it might be. The format can vary. In addition, there will also on occasion be three-team mini-tournaments or different game experiences tried out for development purposes. These may include 'bio-banding', where players from across two or even three age groups are organised based on their physical size or perceived physical maturity. The Premier League has also experimented with a few 'uneven' games where it might start 7v7 but then one team is reduced to five players to see how they adapt and deal with it. Most games are played over four periods, usually of 20 minutes each. This gives coaches the chance to share the minutes around their squad. All these factors affecting the organisation of fixtures can be varied by mutual agreement or circumstance, but this gives you a good picture of what you can normally expect.

In addition to the normal games programme there are also Premier League national tournaments for all ages from u9 to u16, initially on a regional basis and then building up to national finals. At u14 and u15 there are cup competitions (at u14 the Albert Phelan Cup and at u15 the Midweek Cup), again on a group or regional basis leading up to national finals. At u18 you have the Premier League Cup and then the blue riband competition for youth football, the FA Youth Cup.

The FA Youth Cup starts its preliminary rounds in mid-August with the extra preliminary round. This is held on a regional basis initially and offers the opportunity for local u18 teams to enter this prestigious competition, which showcases the best u18 talent across the country. The academy u18s join in at a later stage. In this sense, the organisation of the FA Youth Cup mirrors the FA Cup itself.

The great majority of FA Youth Cup games are played midweek under floodlights. Consequently, these early rounds offer scouts the opportunity to catch up on local talent at a time in the season when the midweek floodlit competitions at u14 or u15 have often not yet got going. In many clubs these early rounds of the FA Youth Cup are covered by academy scouts, although in others they might be picked up by grassroots scouts or a combination of both. Most scouts regard these games as enjoyable, competitive and worth watching, and they are a good showcase of local talent.

Most clubs – and this particularly applies to the bigger academies as they join in the subsequent rounds – will pick their best u18s to play in the FA Youth Cup, such is its historical importance. So if a club has a really good u17 or u18 who usually plays in their u21s or is even in and around the first-team squad, it is likely that they will play in the FA Youth Cup as the club will want to field the strongest possible team.

As the competition progresses, the surviving teams will often play the quarter-final or semi-final at their first-team ground, and by then you can usually expect a lot of scouts to be watching. If a non-league or lower-league academy has a good run in the FA Youth Cup, then again you can expect a lot of scouts will be scheduling their games in to watch.

The larger Category 2 and Category 1 academies will operate u21 teams, and again most of these fixtures are played midweek. This level of football can be a bit problematic and perhaps has yet to find its real role.

The better u17 and u18 players in an academy will often play u21 football. In addition, you have the first-year or maybe even second-year pros who have not gone out on loan. Increasingly we see that young players, particularly at the bigger clubs, are not so patient as in the past, perhaps, and want to get into first-team football or go on loan pretty much as soon as they get past u18.[6] So it can at times seem that u21 football is a mix of young players playing up and older players who do not really want to be there. The football can at times seem a bit insipid and lack a real edge. This is not always the case, but it is a common complaint from scouts.

A few years ago I can recall hearing Neil Bath, then head of youth development at Chelsea and now Director of Football Operations there, say that the solution would be for the Premier League to offer a winning prize of £5m for the top u21 league. This would certainly focus the minds of the participating clubs and may be one way to make it matter more.

Having said that, scouts do regularly attend u21 games, and at times there can be more scouts than fans in attendance! The bigger clubs are tracking the better u17 and u18 players playing up, and the smaller clubs

---

6   All the rules are in 'Youth Development Rules' 2023/24', July 23 via www.premierleague.com

are looking out for who might be released at the end of their first- or second-year pro contracts, or who might be available for a loan.

Okay, so you have found your fixture and you have got in to watch the game. You have the criteria that your club work by in terms of assessing the player (covered in Chapter Three) and you have reported as required (covered in Chapter Five). Let's assume that you identify a player of interest and they are signed to another academy. Let's assume your club has done their cross-checking and the conclusion is that this is a player you would like to sign. What happens now?

Generally the rules are the same for signed young players aged u9–u18 as they are for adult players. If a player is signed at a club, you cannot approach them (or their parents) to get them to come to your club. If you do this and are found out, your club can be severely punished, as this would be an 'illegal approach'.

Players aged u9 to u12 usually sign for one season at a time. At u13 it is usually a two-year registration, as it is at u15, then from u17 you are into the scholar ages and signing professional from 17 years of age. When it comes to the end of any of these registrations, parents can decide they want the player to leave the academy they are signed to. Let's call this 'Academy A'.

The rules tell us that by the third Saturday in May every academy must send their u9–u11 players a formal notice saying whether they intend to retain or release the player with effect from the first Saturday in June. This also applies to the u12 and u14 players, who will be given notice of an intended two-year registration. If the player is being released, they can look elsewhere after receiving that notice. In fact, many academies will let players know earlier than this – often in March or April – to give them time to find other clubs. At this stage many scouts get very busy – checking their notes, asking contacts who is being released and trying to get in quickly before any other clubs.

But if the parent and player want away and the club want to retain them and have notified them as such, then they have to notify the club in writing before the first Saturday in June that they intend to go elsewhere. This is known as 'putting their letter in'.

Let's say that the player decides to leave Academy A. The academy has notified the parents that they want to retain the player. The parents write to say they want away – they 'put their letter in'. The player can go elsewhere. Let's say they go to train at Academy B – a rival club. If Academy B wants to sign the player they can do so, but the Premier League will check everything through to make sure there were no illegal approaches before the due date. This means no personal telephone or text contact from anyone associated with Academy B that in any way could be seen as them inducing or encouraging the player to leave Academy A when the time comes.

Academy A might suspect Academy B of 'tapping the player up', and formally complains to the Premier League. The Premier League will ask all parties for evidence and information anyway, but basically, if allegations are made, the onus is on Academy B to prove they or anyone associated with them did not break the rules. Scouts can be asked to produce their phone records. If they refuse, the Premier League may take this as an admission of wrongdoing! If the records show text messages or phone calls between the scout and a parent or family member of the player, the Premier League may well assume the worst. But the scout may know the family or have other reasons to contact them. However, it is up to them to prove it was not a tap-up.

I must say the stringency of these rules and the very harsh penalties and interpretation of them have led a lot of scouts in many clubs to only use encrypted message systems – such as WhatsApp – for all messaging and discussions around players, even internally as a recruitment team.

If you are Academy B and you have identified a player in Academy A as being of interest, then you will want to know whether they are interested in coming across to you before these key dates, so you can plan your summer recruitment. If you are the parent and are thinking of leaving Academy A, you would want to know whether Academy B is interested in your son before you 'put your letter in'.

You can see where this leads scouts and clubs – and parents too, in fact. Football, like many spheres, runs on gossip. If an academy player is not happy and wants away, then the news spreads around very quickly. Ideally, you would want to find out everything you can about the player – their family, their background, what school they go to, everything. Find out if they are interested in coming to your academy. So you do your 'due diligence'. You use your network and dig for info. You might be adept at trawling social media for information discreetly. Signing a player is such a big commitment for an academy that they will want full information on a player of interest, especially if there is compensation to be paid, which we will discuss later.

You can see how all this leads into the murkier side of scouting. However, there is another route. If Academy B wants a player from Academy A, they can 'go in the front door'. In other words, they formally contact Academy A and say, 'We would like to talk to the parents of this player because we want to sign him.' Academy A may say, 'Okay, let's talk about compensation.' Or they may say, 'No, thanks, not interested.' If so, they are not required to tell the parents of the player involved about this approach if they do not want to. This hardly seems fair and, in any case, these things have a way of getting out anyway, so it is perhaps not a wise road for Academy A to go down. Academy A might talk to the parents, and they may say they are quite happy where they are and do not want to leave for Academy B. That is fair enough, of course.

Academy B may ask whether they can have the player come in for a couple of weeks to train with them. If they are a bigger club than Academy A, then they may agree, thinking they could get some good compensation, or at worst give their player some interesting experience. This happens quite often. For example, a couple of years ago when Ethan Ampadu was in his u16 year at Exeter City it became clear that a lot of clubs were watching him. He was already playing quite regularly in Exeter's first team. They saw the writing on the wall and presumably felt they may as well cash in as much as they could. With Exeter's cooperation and usually with a member of their staff in attendance, Ethan visited interested clubs such as Arsenal, Manchester United and Chelsea. Ethan eventually chose Chelsea, and Exeter got a couple of million out of the deal when it was eventually settled.

However, many academies will resist such approaches for a player to come in and train, preferring for clubs to make an offer if they are interested. I am not sure this is always in the best interests of the player – or the host academy, in fact. If the player wants away and hears of this interest, they may resent the host academy standing in their way.

You can, of course, understand the smaller academies becoming frustrated at losing their best prospects. Many will try to hold on until the player gets to scholar and first pro deal stage and maybe gets in some first-team appearances, as by then the potential fee has gone beyond the academies compensation scheme and may well have increased significantly.

Let's assume that either the two academies involved reach an agreement or it goes to the Premier League compensation process. What sort of money are we talking about? Well, it depends on what category of academy the host academy is and how long the player has been registered there. The basic structure is:[7]

---

7   As at July 2023.

Age Group:	Category 1	Category 2	Category 3
u9	£5,000	£5,000	£5,000
u10	£10,000	£8,750	£7,500
u11	£15,000	£12,500	£10,000
u12	£45,000	£30,000	£15,000
u13	£60,000	£40,000	£20,000
u14 to u16	£80,000 pa	£50,000 pa	£25,000 pa

So, if our player is u13 and has been at Academy A since u9 and Academy A is a Category 3 academy, then the compensation will be:

	£
1 year at u9	5,000
1 year at u10	7,500
1 year at u11	10,000
1 year at u12	15,000
1 year at u13	20,000
Total	**57,500**

This compensation is meant to help make up for the years of training and investment that Academy A has put into the player. In practice it can be a starting point for discussion, and if Academy B wants to have a good future relationship with Academy A and/or does not want any acrimonious dispute that the Premier League would then get involved in, they may offer more.

From u16 upwards the system gets more complicated and there are follow-on payments for first-team appearances and so on, and it is usually much more of an 'open', non-formulaic calculation, much more akin to the negotiations around a senior player.

This gives you the basic idea of how the system works and how much – in ballpark terms – it costs for an academy to sign a player from another academy. If the player is released, of course, then there is no compensation payable.

This is what your scouting at academy level can lead to. Any moves are more often at the end of the season, although it can be done mid-season by agreement. But this is why most academy scouting teams build up their reports and targets through the season, leading up to around April when the identification of priority targets becomes more focused. Any discussion between clubs is usually at head of academy recruitment level, again depending on the structure of the club.

Academy scouting brings you a decent standard of football to watch, normally at good grounds even though you are not always greeted with open arms and are usually out in the elements. You will get to meet some great scouts if you are fortunate. I have made some good friends over many years. There is a small group of professional scouts that I would trust with sharing information on players. When it works like that it can be mutually beneficial, but not all academy scouts, in my experience, will share information. Some want it all one way.

Similarly, some clubs are welcoming and helpful and I have built up good contacts in several key clubs in my region over the years. This is all part of building your network. It is a different network from grassroots scouting but just as important.

Some scouts find that the long process of identifying players of interest, usually building up through an entire season, can feel like a lot of work for little identifiable reward. This can be so compared to grassroots scouting, where if you like a player you may be able to push for them to come in straight away on trial. Some scouts feel grassroots scouting gives more of an immediate return. On the other hand, the better standard of football that you are watching week in, week out is an attraction or preference for many academy scouts. It is about personal preference, and if you get the chance to try both you can find out where you feel most comfortable and engaged.

Conner Agar is a bright scout who has worked for Portsmouth, AFC Bournemouth and Manchester City. The move up into top-level academy scouting was something of a step-change in several ways for him, including how video scouting, which we shall discuss in more depth later, became a more significant part of his job:

> I had a huge shock and shift in how I had to work when moving into the elite side of academy football and watching the best players around the country. Access to games online was very easy and allowed for more coverage sat in the comfort of your own home. You begin to adapt rather quickly as this allows you to be more productive.

We see that different types of scouting require some of the same skills but some different ones, too. Academy scouting has its interests and merit but is not for everyone.

See Chris's video on 'Do Academies Break Hearts?':

Chapter Eight

First-Team and Video Scouting

I HAVE stressed throughout this book that a key element of good scouting is knowing what level you are scouting for. This is an obvious one but overlooked by many scouts, as I have said, because watching your own team or teams is not always the priority it should be.

This is never truer than in first-team scouting at any level. If you are scouting for a first team, you really need to know several vital things, regardless of how good you are at assessing players generally. Firstly, you absolutely must know the level of football that you are recruiting for. If you are working for a Championship club, for example, then you must know the Championship inside out. This means you must immerse yourself in that level, watch a lot of games in that division and understand the clubs involved and the current trends. Even if you are mostly looking at players at other levels – u21, League One or whatever – to recruit into the Championship, you must be really comfortable that you know what players will thrive in the Championship and why. There really is no shortcut to this and it applies whether you are scouting in the Premier League or the Isthmian League. We can call this 'the setting' that you are working in.

Secondly, just as vital, you must know exactly what your first-team manager/head coach (I will refer to this person as head coach from here on) really wants in terms of the type of player he is seeking. So if the priority is a striker – what sort of striker? Someone who can go in behind with pace or someone with great hold-up play? What are the 'must have' attributes? We can call this 'the style' you are looking for.

Thirdly, you must know what the club's recruitment strategy is. Are they looking for instant results where the age of the player is not a key consideration but a proven track record at that level is? Or are they only interested in younger players with potential sell-on market value in the future? We can call this 'the strategy' you are following.

To be fair, in most clubs these three issues – *setting*, *style* and *strategy* – will be explained clearly or be self-evident to any new first-team scout as they are the cornerstone of the recruitment process in practice.

However, as a scout these are the three issues you must have covered and feel clear about for you to do your job properly. Like I said in Chapter Two: you need to know your elephant.

We start with information, which for bigger clubs comes in the form of data. So, for example, if you are working for a Premier League club, there are numerous 'givens'. Your club will have a significant provision of recruitment data that provides context for your work. Some clubs are more data-driven than others and various clubs may use different types of data in different ways. However, no Premier League club operates their recruitment without data nowadays. So, it is no longer a matter of 'if' data plays a part but 'how' it plays a part. That ship has long sailed, and over the last 20 years the growth of data in football and its effect on the game has been well documented, and frankly is now blatantly obvious.[8]

The top clubs now either buy in data from the big players such as Opta or Wyscout or produce their own – often a combination of the two in practice. Data provision is a key part of the components that a big club needs to bring together, and they understand

---

8   There are a lot of books out now covering data in football. *The Numbers Game* by Chris Anderson and David Sally, Penguin Books 2013, was a key contribution and *Expected Goals* by Rory Smith, Harper Collins, 2022 is a good summary so far.

this importance, although may approach it differently. Arsenal bought Stat DNA, the US-based football data analytics company in 2012, for around £2m to enhance their data process. The big clubs are hiring the top data management talent from all sorts of different backgrounds.

You can look at the data world in football as a sort of pyramid. At the base level all clubs from the Premier League down to the top few steps of the non-league pyramid will be routinely filming their games. The technology to have an analyst then 'clip and code' the footage – that is, identify the snippets of action for each player so they can be brought together or easily watched without going through the whole game – is cheap and widely available. Coaches and players will routinely review this footage to identify what a player did in a game, and perhaps what they did not do.

Slightly further up the data pyramid is the capacity to measure a further range of performance measures such as distance covered by the team as a whole and by each player, passes made, tackles and so forth – usually by using GPS tracking systems. Another step further towards the top of the data pyramid would be the capacity to look at more detailed information such as runs at full pace, noting speed and distance covered and so forth.

All this data so far is very dependent on context – a player might have a 90 per cent success rate on passes, which sounds positive, but if 70 per cent of those were backwards or sideways would it be so impressive? Therefore, at the top of the data pyramid is the increasingly sophisticated data that identifies the extent that a player positively affects the game. There is a keen search on for the key performance indicators that will gauge likely success in a game. This might be in terms of 'packing', which I described in Chapter Three – how passes 'take out' opposing players from the play – or passes into a specific area such as the last third of the pitch or opposing penalty area, or tackles and interceptions made in key areas and so on. This will all depend on what the head coach and his team believe are the most important metrics. The whole field of 'expected goals', where a game is analysed to estimate how many goals 'should' have been scored given the play, as opposed to how many were actually scored, is a good example of this development of more sophisticated data. The higher up the data pyramid you go the more difficult and costly it becomes to collect the data.

However, all this is performance data and will be mostly collected and analysed within each club. The emerging big data companies operating in football soon realised that some clubs would buy this sort of performance data from them rather than slog through and produce it themselves, and crucially, where recruitment is concerned, would be really interested in comparative data. This allows you to compare players according to the data you believe is important – players from other clubs and, indeed, leagues. Now we are beginning to get into the realm of recruitment data; that is, comparative player information used to help the recruitment process.

Where recruitment is concerned, what sort of data are we talking about? Again it is largely that reflected in the data pyramid I have described, but it is organised in a database that allows you to put in certain criteria and then have a list of players that meet that criteria and, thus, compare players. If your club is looking for a right-back that has pace, good general athleticism, a good injury record, is able to play in the Championship for a team aiming for the play-offs, able to play in a four and as a wing-back, aged in their early 20s so you have a resale value with a likely transfer fee of £x million or less, and in the last two years of a contract, then you can set those as your search parameters and ask your recruitment analyst or your data company to produce you a list of the top ten candidates. You can also compare candidates against your current right-back's data. In practice, most big clubs have rolling 'top tens' of players of interest in all positions.

As you can see, we are now in the realms not just of *setting* – Championship play-offs standard, for example, but *style* – quick, athletic, with good touch and able to play in a four or as a wing-back – and *strategy* – age, contract situation, likely transfer fee. We will talk more about these specific aspects later, but for now the point is that recruitment data can assist in filtering and prioritising players.

Obviously, at the top level – Premier League, let's say – the scope is worldwide and the data generally available at a price. The big data companies have teams of analysts, often in lower-wage countries such as the Philippines or India, working hard coding games by watching videos and using special keyboards. Gradually we are seeing more and more of this able to be done digitally or by process rather than manually. As this capacity to analyse games via video and produce the performance stats automatically increases, then the data will be more widely available and cheaper. More sophisticated measures such as 'packing' data will become more widely available, for example. Perhaps more clubs will share data, which enables a lot of innovation and new ideas to take hold too.

As you go down the football levels there is less access either to home-grown data, with fewer analysts working and less access to comparative data, as not many clubs can afford to buy this sort of service. There are also fewer games widely available to watch on video to start the process off. So, for example, National League games – the top level, Step One of 'non-league football' – are available on commercial sites such as In-Stat. However, at the next level down, National League South and North, it becomes more difficult to access videos, although more clubs do share them via their own cheap subscription services or even YouTube or other platforms.

Consequently, as you go down the levels into non-league, more of the recruitment comparative process must be done via live scouting. If you are a scout for a National League South club or below and your task is to find a right-back, you will need to use your networks and your own information and scouting. You might find it useful to have, if not various 'top tens' in all positions, maybe 'top threes', all according to your setting, style and strategy.

A lot of this will be very familiar to those football fans who are keen on 'Football Manager' and other data-based manager simulation games. The whole process of players being assessed and scored and then compared and filtered does largely mirror what happens in real life, although, as we know, the data is now much more sophisticated in the real world. The 'Football Manager' generation of scouts and would-be scouts are already halfway there with this data-driven approach. In fact, I believe the 'Football Manager' database was at one time acquired by one of the big data companies as it was seen to be so useful. Of course, online games lack the reality of watching games live or dealing with the often complex nature of the athletes and other people that you will be dealing with. Nevertheless, they are realistic enough in their way.

You as a scout will need to decide where and how you do your live scouting and how to make use of your inevitably limited time most productively. Neil Sillett is an extremely experienced scout and former head of recruitment. Neil believes you need a mix of data and live scouting. 'In my opinion,' he says, 'the mix of trained eye and analytics is the most efficient way. The experts can see behaviours exhibited in a game, which data and analytics may not, and the desire, hunger and attitude of a player needs to be witnessed first-hand.'

When I was managing in non-league, I would do a lot of the scouting myself although I did in time have one or two scouts to help. I remember when I was managing Willenhall Town, my first management gig, I went to see Graham Allner, who was manager of Kidderminster Harriers in what was then called the Conference, now the National League. They were a couple of divisions above us and doing very well. As a young coach and manager, I would routinely try to contact experienced managers around me and try to learn from them. I invariably found them receptive and helpful. In this way, such coaches and managers as Dario Gradi, Neil Baker, Dave Sexton, Bobby Hope, Pete Amos and Barry Stobart were all very helpful to me along the way. I would encourage all young managers to reach out and get guidance and advice from more experienced people they respect, and young scouts can too. I have invariably found people helpful, and the same goes in the scouting world.

I went to see Graham in his portacabin office at Aggborough, Kidderminster's ground. We talked about our own scouting. He advised moving my Tuesday night training to Monday as there were routinely more games to watch on a Tuesday night. As a non-league part-time manager, if my team were not training or playing then I was out watching games. 'You scout for tomorrow,' Graham advised, and he meant you are watching games, noting players of interest and then when you need that particular position filled you can check your notes or memory and say, 'Yes, there was that lad at club X, let's watch him again.' Both Graham and I would go on later to manage Cheltenham Town, funnily enough, and I would often see him on the Midlands non-league circuit, scouting for tomorrow. In a way, I suppose he was pointing me towards having my own shortlist of players of interest in various positions, as mentioned previously.

Recruitment in football of all sorts can seem to be in panic mode at times. A rumour suddenly circulates that a player is unhappy at his club, or an agent contacts you and says player X wants away or whatever. Then it can be hectic urgent action trying to get info together, summarising reports and making rushed decisions. In transfer windows, or leading up to them, this is particularly the case. The big desperation is not to miss out to a rival for potentially key players, although players can suddenly become more interesting when you know that a rival wants them!

The key is to prepare properly and to have and trust a robust filtering and assessment system so you have target lists that you absolutely believe in. If you prepare properly, you can make better decisions in frantic times – if you hold your nerve and trust your process.

The Setting

As I have mentioned, if you are working for a Championship club you will often find yourself watching other levels when scouting players. Consequently, judging whether a player would be successful at a different level is a key skill for scouts. It applies throughout scouting in many cases. If you are a grassroots scout and scouting for a pro academy, then you are judging how well a player could translate their performance to a different level.

When I was doing academy scouting for Chelsea, a top Category 1 academy, of course, I would watch Category 3 games and be so aware that what I was scouting players into was going to be very different from what I was watching. The games at Category 1 clubs are generally quicker, at a higher technical level and require better physical conditioning. So, the ability to judge whether a player could step up in levels and perform well is a key attribute of a scout. In addition, you will sometimes be trying to decide whether a player could play at a different level but not necessarily a higher level. For example, you might be watching a u21 game on behalf of a Championship club and trying to judge whether this player could move from the technical but often lightweight setting of u21 football into the demanding Championship level.

A fine example of the challenges of judging a player from a very different level would be Moises Caicedo. After just 25 games in Ecuador's Serie A, at the age of 19 he was bought by Brighton in February 2021, allegedly for £4m. He had played for Ecuador's national team but did not make his senior debut there until October 2020, although he was involved in the World Cup in November 2020. Nevertheless, it was a huge leap to imagine he might become a Premier League player.

I have heard it said that when trying to assess whether a player can move up a series of levels you look for what their standout attributes are. You can look for 'world-class attributes' that would be effective at any level. This might be their pace, for example, or ability to break up play, and you may feel that this player does that so well he could do it at a higher level. It was interesting to note that most of the scouting of Caicedo was on video too! Brighton paid their £4m, he came and was loaned out to a Belgian club before coming back to Brighton, where he made an immediate impact in the Premier League. So much so that in the summer of 2023 top clubs were vying for him and he eventually joined Chelsea, allegedly in a deal that would be worth more than £100m. It was not only a fantastic return for Brighton on their

£4m but a great vindication of their ability to assess whether a player could translate his performance to a very different level of football.

There are other examples of players who have translated well. Jamie Vardy is a well-known example of a player who missed out on pro football the first time round but then came via non-league into the lower league levels before working his way up to winning the Premier League with Leicester City and playing for England. If you look at Vardy, you would say the top attributes that stand out as transferable up the levels were his pace and his finishing. There are some rare players who just seem able to score goals at any level.

Another example of a player who was identified as being able to perform up the levels was Andy Robertson, Liverpool's left-back. Robertson started his career at Queen's Park in Scotland, graduating from their youth set-up (having previously been at Celtic but released at u15, apparently because he was considered 'too small') into their first team at age 18. He then moved to Dundee United and did well there, winning his first international cap and being named PFA Scotland Young Player of the Year. In July 2014 he joined Hull City (for £2.85m) and had three seasons with them, getting relegated from the Premier League, promoted and then relegated again. Liverpool took the plunge, signing him for what looks now like a bargain fee of allegedly £8m in July 2017. At the time of writing he has played almost 200 times for the club, including winning the Champions League and the Premier League, and he picked up an MBE along the way!

So what was it that Robertson did that suggested he could step up? Stan Ternent was Hull City's chief scout when they signed him and has referred to the decision as a 'no-brainer', citing Robertson's determination and ability to overcome setbacks, such as his Celtic release. Robertson was always quick, bright and worked hard. He has always been a real competitor. These are the elements that have persuaded scouts that he can step further up each time and indeed is now regarded as one of the best left-backs in the world.

What elements of play should we as scouts look for that are translatable? The game gets quicker as you progress up the levels, so not just pace, but speed of thought is going to be key. We have mentioned finishing already. That coolness in front of goal, that sense of composure and clinical finishing is very translatable – but very rare too!

There are some areas where it may not be realistic to hope a player can step up. You can expect a player's touch and even game awareness to improve with better coaching, but by how much? A player's ability to make decisions quicker or play simpler football with fewer touches can be difficult to estimate when they are playing in a slower-paced game where they do not need to show those attributes, and are they habits that will be hard to break?

Judging a player's ability to move their setting can be very difficult. For every Caicedo, there are probably ten or more who do not thrive at the higher level. Judging whether a player can adapt or change is tough, particularly with younger players who may still be growing or changing physical shape.

I recall being sent to watch Dele Alli in 2014 when he was playing regularly in the MK Dons first team at age 17 or so. He was quite sturdy, playing central midfield and had confidence and a good touch, but was not particularly mobile. A lot of top clubs were watching him then – I recall Brendan Rodgers, then Liverpool manager, was at the game I attended. In my report I said that while it was good that he was playing first-team football at that age and he had the ability, I felt we had at least two similar-aged midfielders in the academy – Ruben Loftus-Cheek and Lewis Baker – that were better prospects. In February 2015 Tottenham bought him and he went on to have a few great seasons with them, under Mauricio Pochettino in particular. I remember in April 2018 he scored two goals against Chelsea at Stamford Bridge, giving Spurs their first win there for 28 years! I reflected then on my report from a few years previously. I concluded that I was right, I stood by that view that, at the time, we had better prospects.

Was I wrong? In hindsight, clearly yes, in terms of future development – even discounting Alli's more recent difficulties. But at the time I clearly thought Ruben and Lewis looked better athletes and had more to offer overall. It would be very difficult to estimate how Alli would slim up and sharpen up, and we were not the only club that passed on him, to be fair.

Similarly, I can remember watching Jadon Sancho – a south London boy and Chelsea fan – playing for Watford as a u14. We had heard Manchester City were interested. Sancho played as a central striker and had good touch but was no more than average when I saw him. He did not look like the wiry, clever winger he later became. Once again you have a player growing up who changed shape to an extent and changed style. It is very difficult to forecast those changes. Even once he was at City and more recognisable as the player he is now, I saw him play against us numerous times and each time I felt that Callum Hudson-Odoi was the better player.

So, judging whether a player can thrive in a different setting is difficult. Clearly, identifying what their best attributes are and considering whether these are translatable is the key – as well as intimately understanding the level you are recruiting to.

The Style

As mentioned, you need to know what style of player your head coach is looking for, to be able to scout effectively for them. There is no shortcut to this. It is one of the reasons that many top head coaches have their own 'head scout' included in the entourage of assistants they like to include in their staff team. They want someone who understands what they look for in a player. Head coaches often have clear preferences in the styles of players. Jose Mourinho, for example, is known to prefer strong, athletic players. I noted earlier that his Roma squad last season had a lot of players at 190cm or above! We often say that head coaches reproduce their character in their teams. You can see teams reflect the head coach's personality. Sam Allardyce's teams might be seen as big and strong and very canny. Arsène Wenger's teams were noted for their intelligent play, intelligent passing and so on.

Sometimes a head coach will have a team set up in a certain way and will need a specific player to fit into that style of play or formation. For example, when I was manager of Cheltenham Town I set the team up in a 3-5-2 formation with one of the midfield three being effectively what we would call a No.10, in the hole. I did this for numerous reasons, mainly because of what players we had, but a key part of that was that I wanted to feature a very gifted player called Lee Howells, and I thought that the No.10 role would suit him and bring out the best in this undoubtedly very good player. However, 'Archie', as he was called, got a serious long-term injury and I needed to find a player who could fill a very specific role by that time, that of the creative No.10. We found Paul Chenoweth from Bath City, who was ideal in that role. It was a question of finding the right piece for the puzzle.

Sometimes, of course, and maybe too often, head coaches change and a player who was bought or signed with one head coach's favoured style of play in mind finds themselves now playing for another head coach who has a very different style. The classic example often quoted in this regard is Christian Benteke. Aston Villa signed the 6ft 3in striker in August 2012 from Genk for £7m. Over the next couple of seasons he scored a goal every 2.1 games. He was strong *and* he scored goals. So, in July 2015, Liverpool, with Brendan Rodgers as manager, bought him for £32.5m. But in October 2015 Rodgers was sacked and Jürgen Klopp came in. It became clear that Benteke was not the sort of striker Klopp wanted, as he was developing his Salah–Firmino–Mane front three, so the big, bustling Benteke did not fit. Benteke played 29 times for Liverpool, scoring nine goals (3.2 games per goal).

Another example of a player not fitting the style of a new head coach would be Romelu Lukaku. Another big Belgian striker, Lukaku probably had the best spell of his career to date playing for Inter Milan under the counter-attacking style of Antonio Conte. There Lukaku scored 47 goals in 72 appearances (a goal per 1.5 games). He was bought by Chelsea in August 2021 for around £97.5m. However, under head coach Thomas Tuchel it became clear that a different type of striker was required. Chelsea under Tuchel kept possession well, and strikers were expected to work hard off the ball and link play. Tuchel preferred Timo Werner or Kai Havertz.

Given this hindsight, Lukaku seems a strange signing for Chelsea in that he did not seem to be what the head coach was looking for. Maybe the club felt he could become that but, for whatever reason, it did not work out. We can see that recruitment is something of a fine art at times, along with all the science of data and research. I guess that is because we are ultimately dealing with human beings and how people react together and gel, or don't gel, is not always easy to judge.

However, the overall point here is that knowing the style that the target player is expected to play in is a vital element of targeted productive scouting.

The Strategy

When scouting for a first-team squad, you will not only need to know the recruitment strategy of your club but ideally you should be a part of it in the sense that it should be a team effort to discuss how any strategy should be put into action.

It may be that your focus is required to be short-term. You may be scouting for a non-league team and the remit is straightforward and urgent: 'We need an experienced centre-back, either side, who knows this level and is a leader and organiser.' You may find that the lower level at which you scout, the shorter-term the focus is. At the higher levels the strategy will certainly have a major input from the ownership of the club and reflect the overall business strategy. If your club is expected to compete this season for the Premier League title, then that brings with it some clear requirements for the players you will be looking at. They will invariably need to be proven performers at the top level.

However, if we look across the 'Big 5' leagues in Europe (the Premier League, La Liga in Spain, Ligue 1 in France, the German Bundesliga and Serie A in Italy) we can see some significant differences from one league to another in their recruitment practices. For example, a 2016 report showed that on average across all five leagues 14.5 per cent of recruited players were from their own internal academy, 7.9 per cent were loan signings, 25 per cent were free transfers and 52.6 per cent were paid transfers.[9] However, there were significant variations between the leagues.

The Premier League clubs had only 8.5 per cent from their academies, a very low 3.7 per cent from loans, 16.6 per cent on free transfers and a whopping 71.2 per cent were paid transfers. Yet Ligue 1 had 23.8 per cent from their own academies and 31.8 per cent were free transfers, with only 39.3 per cent being paid transfers. La Liga had 19.2 per cent from their own academies and only 35.6 per cent were paid transfers. The Premier League featured many more international transfers – recruiting 46.8 per cent of players from foreign clubs – yet in Serie A this was only 37.7 per

---

9   'Recruitment strategies throughout Europe', Dr Raffaele Poll et al, *CIES Football Observatory Monthly Report*, Issue 18 – October 2016.

cent. The time players spent at clubs varied across the 'Big 5' too. In the Premier League the average was 2.32 years, while La Liga was 1.69 years.

So we can see a general pattern in that the Premier League recruited more internationally, and had more paid transfers, with longer contracts and more stable squads. This reflects the comparative wealth of the Premier League.

There is a wider point here. Because the Premier League replaced the old First Division of the Football League and is based in England, we think it is a straight successor. In my view it is more realistic to see the Premier League as an international league. In fact, it is the predominant international league, which just happens to be based in the UK. This helps us appreciate the different recruitment patterns of the Premier League. If you are scouting in the Premier League you will generally be covering a lot of international games (probably on video, as we shall discuss), looking at a lot of young players already with good high-level league and international experience. Few Premier League clubs recruit from our League One in practice, or from Scotland or Ireland, come to that.

But within the Premier League itself, there are a variety of recruitment strategies in play as clubs have very different expectations and plans. For example,

Bournemouth and Burnley will usually be looking at different players to Chelsea and Manchester City. So, in the 2016 study, we saw that the four clubs across Europe who recruited players with the most high-level playing experience the previous season were Manchester City, Real Madrid, Manchester United and Chelsea. Bournemouth recruited 7.1 per cent of their players on loan, and Burnley 8 per cent, while Chelsea, Manchester City and Manchester United did not recruit any players on loan. This all makes sense but reflects a varied recruitment landscape within the Premier League. It means that the requirements on scouts will vary too.

Brentford were playing in League One as recently as 2014. They secured their Premier League spot in 2021. Matthew Benham, the owner, comes from a data background in the betting world. It was not surprising that he would be attracted to the new football data world we have described earlier. Brentford focused on unearthing players with real potential from relatively lowly levels. For example, Ollie Watkins was signed from Exeter City in 2017 for £1.8m and later sold to Aston Villa for £28m.

Brighton too, as mentioned, with owner Tony Bloom from a similar background to Benham, have focused their recruitment strategy on signing players they feel have as yet unrealised market value. In fact, Bloom hired Benham in the early 2000s to work for his company Premier Bet, although allegedly the pair later fell out and in practice became rivals, first in the betting world and then the football world. Players such as Ben White, Leo Trossard, Marc Cucurella and, of course, Moises Caicedo have done very well for Brighton, having been signed relatively cheaply and sold at a high profit.

The new Chelsea ownership that took the club over in 2022 have set out their strategy. They clearly want to sign the best young talents from around the world aged 18–21 and then, through loans and coaching, develop them into world-class players. Consequently, they have signed players such as Andrey Santos and Deivid Washington from Brazil who have great potential, but they have also signed relatively young players such as Enzo Fernandez and Moises Caicedo for sums in excess of £100m. They clearly are not just looking to the future but also want some returns now in terms of immediate first-team success, or at least significant improvement, yet they still prefer younger players on long contracts.

All these different approaches will translate into different requirements for players that scouts will be watching. It is obviously very different if you must find a young player with longer-term market value as compared to someone who can come into your first team straight away and make an impact now.

Lower down the leagues and in non-league football, it is increasingly likely that first-team scouting will be less reliant on video scouting – although that is continuing to grow – and more short-term; that is, players for this season or, at most, the coming season. Contracts in non-league tend to be relatively short-term for the most part other than the biggest clubs, and it all reflects a necessarily more focused recruitment requirement. As mentioned, at this level it is again a matter of networks. The scouts who are out and about, in touch with other scouts and football contacts generally, swimming in the waters so to speak, are most likely to hear who is doing well, who is up for a move and so on. The trade papers – the *Football League* and the *Non-League Paper* and their accompanying websites – are invaluable.

Some local papers will focus on non-league too, although not so many. When I was managing in non-league in the Midlands in the 90s the 'bible' was the *Sports Argus* – the 'pink 'un', which hit the streets at about 6.30pm on a Saturday. Not only did it cover the results from that afternoon, but it also had excellent background and gossip features on the local non-league scene, which was a remarkable and priceless service for non-league in the region. For years I would get regular phone calls from the lead journalist on this section – Colin Stoner, who was an intelligent and very well-informed source of non-league information. The *Argus* would be pored over by non-league people, from players to directors, managers and coaches every week. It was sure to feature in the conversations that those people had about the game. It ran from 1897 until 2006, when the last standalone edition came out. It continues as a pullout section of the Saturday and Monday editions of the *Birmingham Mail*.

Video Scouting

Video scouting has grown remarkably over the last five years. Partly this was due to the lockdown of the Covid pandemic. During that time clubs struggled to find games for scouts to watch. Having said that, many clubs laid their scouts off. For those who, like Chelsea, stuck by their staff during that period, the challenge was to find videos for scouts to watch, as there were no live games for a long period.

At first-team level in the Premier League and other major leagues, this was not so much of a problem, as match videos were widely available, including through platforms such as Instat. For the lower leagues, and certainly for academy football, it was much more of a struggle but did lead in practice to several informal arrangements to share videos between academies. This was already long overdue and surely it cannot be long before a cooperative platform is found to facilitate the sharing of videos between academies on a regulated and systematic basis. However, connections were made, and video scouting continues to grow.

Partly, of course, this is due to the increasing availability and affordability of the technology, such as VEO cameras and others. This means that virtually all academies and an increasing number of grassroots clubs can afford to film games. More and more grassroots clubs are finding ways to put them on some sort of shared platform, be it the club website or their own YouTube channel or whatever.

So, scouting through video has become a familiar and notable feature of modern scouting. It is now so prevalent at first-team level at the bigger clubs that something like 90–95 per cent of first-team scouting is being done by video. Given the international focus of the higher leagues, this is a practical step that is both cost- and time-efficient. I was told Brighton saved about £2m a season in costs when they switched to predominantly video scouting at first-team level, and other big clubs will have had similar experiences.

However, video scouting is not without its challenges. At the highest level, even though the quality of the filming is good, often featuring multiple cameras, if it is broadcast material you still only see part of the play. If I am focusing on a specific player – doing a 'portrait' report as mentioned earlier – then I do not always want to follow the ball. I want to see what positions the player takes up when the ball is down the other end of the pitch, for example, and what movements they make on transitions when possession changes hands, and so on. A video is not usually going to show you that. If you are watching a goalkeeper, you want to follow their starting position, for example, and you will not usually see that. So videos are a good way to get a general impression of a game and a good focus on when the player is near the ball.

Further down the levels, the quality of the video can become an issue. Usually filmed on one camera and often from a high, distant perspective, the quality varies hugely. This is particularly true of academy and grassroots games on video. So, again, we can use these videos for a general impression but not the detail. Where reporting is concerned at the academy level, where you do not usually get team sheets and some academies do not even wear shirt numbers, identifying individual players on video can be a nightmare. If you know who you are looking for or looking at then they can be a useful medium to do a 'portrait' report on that specific player, but without a team sheet and usually without sound it is virtually impossible to do 'thumbnail' reports.

Where video does impact on a scout's work in addition to games, however, is through the 'clipping' of videos to produce a highlights reel of a specific player's impact on a game. This is routine at the higher levels and in academy football too, and helps give you a useful summary of a specific player's performance on the ball in any given game or series of games. Again, for me, it is not a substitute to thoroughly scouting a player in the wider context of the game, but it is helpful. It may be done by an analyst, but if you as a scout are adept at this, then it is another string to your professional bow.

Recruitment teams will regularly ask scouts to watch videos in addition to their own live games to form a variety of views on a particular player. Most clubs will require a certain number of views by different scouts to increase the 'validity' of the overall assessment of a player. This is partly because it is human nature to make your mind up about a player and then seek affirmation of your own views through subsequent games. This 'confirmation bias' is natural, and something scouts need to be aware of is to try to stay as objective as they can for as long as they can. However, when you are paid to give your opinions on players it is very difficult not to start reaching for conclusions early on! We will look at various biases in more detail in Chapter Twelve. Awareness of these issues is one of the reasons recruitment teams increasingly adopt a team approach, seeking to cross-check opinions and a depth of perspectives. Scouting has become a team game.

One further aspect of the video clips of players that will impact a scout's work is being sent videos and clips of a player. This may come from the player, a parent of a child or the agent of a more senior player. Every scout can expect to get some of these. I will look at some of the practical issues in the later chapter on parents, but I will say here that amid all the poor-quality videos of poor-quality games you will occasionally get a sight of a player who sparks your interest. So I would say to scouts, do not be dismissive of the stream of videos and clips being sent your way. I must say that I try to watch them all. You never know.

Finally, in this review of first-team scouting, I should mention the emerging role of the 'director of football' or 'sporting director', or other similar titles that means a senior person who often now oversee and drives the recruitment at first-team level and even beyond. The model of a 'director of football' or 'technical director' or whatever, who is often responsible for senior recruitment but also the general oversight of football development and operations in a club, has been noticeable in the UK over the last ten years. It has been in use longer in Europe and elsewhere.

In practice, there is a great range of practical arrangements in different clubs. It will depend on how the interface between the club's ownership and the football delivery is structured. In some clubs the owner might be the chairperson, for example, and take a keen direct interest in first-team recruitment. In the bigger clubs there will be more of a structure, possibly featuring the 'director of football' role or equivalent. Again, the extent to which the head coach is involved in recruitment will vary. Traditionally, an Alex Ferguson or Arsène Wenger style of manager were very much involved in first-team recruitment. The 'big-name' head coaches such as Jose Mourinho, Thomas Tuchel, Jürgen Klopp or Antonio Conte are not going to work without a major say in first-team recruitment and often have their own people in key positions within the recruitment structure. However, the more European norm of a head coach whose job is basically to make the best of the players the ownership can provide, is also in evidence. In many cases it will be a mix of the two. Head coaches are very focused on the next game, inevitably, and once a season is underway they simply do not have time or space to become too involved in recruitment practice.

The effect of these different structures on you as a scout might well show in who you report to. Do you report to the head coach or the director of football, or maybe a head scout or head of recruitment? In an academy it will be through to an academy head of recruitment, although, again in the bigger academies, this will usually be through teams focusing on grassroots or academy scouting, or even specific age groups.

We are seeing an increase in the use of 'position-specific' scouting; that is, scouts who will focus on strikers or goalkeepers or whatever position. This is an interesting idea, presumably seeking more focus and specialist knowledge, and it will be interesting to see whether it becomes more widespread. I think there is already an acceptance that goalkeeping is specialist enough to require goalkeeping scouts, just as there are goalkeeping coaches.

First-team scouting can seem glamorous. It is probably the most visible scouting at the top end of any club. However, it is not without its challenges, as we have seen, and it is increasingly focused on video scouting and can be insecure as head coaches come and go. Yet, go to any pub or social gathering where football fans are gathered and it seems there are a great many people who believe they know what their first team needs and who they do not need. Opinions are cheap. If you are paid to give them, be prepared to work.

Follow the link to see me talking about video scouting:

Chapter Nine

Opposition Scouting

MOST OF the scouting we have covered so far focuses essentially on assessing an individual player – how good are they? Are they good enough for us? However, another key area of the scouting spectrum is opposition scouting – sometimes termed technical scouting – which focuses on the performances of a whole team, usually one that your team will be facing soon.

Some of the skills of a scout in the areas we have covered so far – grassroots scouting, academy scouting and first-team scouting – are clearly transferrable to opposition scouting. These include an in-depth understanding of the game, for example. However, opposition scouting also requires an appreciation of the wider picture of performance in a game, which means the ability to understand formations, patterns of play and how a team adapts to different problems and challenges.

The Differing Approaches of Head Coaches

The first thing we should consider is the differing approaches of head coaches to games, in the sense of how interested they are in how the opposition plays. After all, it is likely to be the head coach that determines what information they require from you on the opposition and they will have their own way of working and analysing.

In his book, *The Mixer*, which traces the different tactical approaches adopted in the Premier League, Michael Cox compares the approaches of Sir Alex Ferguson with Manchester United and Kevin Keegan with Newcastle United in their tussle for the Premier League title in 1995/96:

> … Newcastle never discussed team shape.
>
> Keegan had a similarly relaxed attitude towards opponents. Alex Ferguson was increasingly adjusting small details to counter an opponent's strengths and provided specific information on their weaknesses.
>
> But Keegan wouldn't mention Newcastle's upcoming opponents in training and would simply read out the opposition's team sheet in

the dressing room shortly before the warm-up.[10]

So clearly you would have a very different job to do as an opposition scout if you had been working for Ferguson as compared to Keegan – in fact, Keegan probably wouldn't employ you anyway! However, even with Keegan, as the season drew to a fraught and tense climax he did make one or two adjustments to Newcastle's approach in specific games.

It can be argued that things have moved on and evolved, and it is hard to imagine any head coach in the current Premier League – or other top leagues – not employing opposition scouts. But what does remain true is that some coaches will determine that their team will go out and play their game and try to impose it on the opposition – Arsène Wenger's Arsenal would be a classic example of this – whereas others will adjust their team's game depending on who they are playing – Jose Mourinho would be an example of this approach. Most modern coaches will adopt a hybrid approach: they will want to play the way that suits their team where they can, but will want to appreciate and counteract the opposition's strengths and exploit their weaknesses along the way.

---

10 *The Mixer: The Story of Premier League Tactics, from Route One to False Nines*, Michael Cox, Harper Collins, 2017.

Those coaches who largely set up a counter-attacking team will place even greater emphasis on researching the opposition. Jose Mourinho is the usual example quoted here, although to an extent you could include Antonio Conte in that too.

In his book on the 2021/22 season, Pep Lijnders, Jürgen Klopp's assistant at Liverpool, wrote about Arsène Wenger coming to visit the Liverpool training ground early in that season. As he watched training, Wenger said, 'The amount of specific information about your next game is incredible.'[11] Lijnders explains how they were approaching each game and adjusting and focusing their training on how they wanted to play their next opponent. All this was based, of course, on information from their head of opposition analysis, Greg Mathieson, and his team. The book is essentially a diary of that season, and I would recommend it as a vivid portrait of the detail that goes into preparing and coaching a top-level team, the extent and range of the staff team that is needed and how they each contribute. In the space of their first three games (newly promoted Norwich, who were a good technical team; Burnley with their long ball and emphasis on second balls; Chelsea, then European champions under Thomas

---

11 *Intensity*, Pep Lijnders, Reach Sport, 2022.

Tuchel) – 'a season in three games' as Lijnders says – you can read how Liverpool analysed their opponents' strengths and weaknesses, then adjusted their own approach and tactics while keeping to their overall season theme of counter-pressing and intensity and seeking to play to their own strengths at the same time.

So if you are tasked with analysing an opposition, you will now be able to gather a lot of data even before you start looking at specific games, at the higher levels of the game at least – 'the research phase'. You will then watch and analyse the opposition – and we will go into how you might do that – in 'the analysis phase'. Whichever way you approach it, your 'product' will consist of relaying your findings to the head coach and his coaching team, and maybe directly to the players, in some form or another – 'the reporting phase'.

The Reporting Phase

Let's deal with this last phase first because it sets a context for all the other work you do and how we are going to look at and explain that work.

At the top levels of the game – probably right down to senior non-league now – the reports produced on opposition scouting will invariably be based on video examples of systems, patterns of play and so on. This is obviously much more of a digestible medium than a written report. This hinges, of course, on the availability of video but, as we have noted in an earlier chapter, this is improving and stretching through the game all the time. It is within the basic analyst skillset to clip and present such information. In addition to that, or lower down the football pyramid in place of that, there will be PowerPoint or similar slides showing the examples diagrammatically.

It may well be that the scout, either individually or working with an analyst, compiles a significant chunk of data and analysis, including stats, game examples and the full range of opposition analysis, and this is edited down for the head coach and staff, and maybe then edited down further for the players as a group or as individuals. The key is to be selective and identify the key information for the specific people involved. Again a lot of this will hinge on the head coach's attitude towards the opposition as set out at the beginning of this chapter.

When Jose Mourinho took over at Chelsea in 2004 each player was presented with a dossier on their forthcoming individual opponent and was expected to absorb this. The next day – the day before the game – there would be a collective discussion led by Mourinho and his staff, including Andre Villas-Boas, who was his opposition scout in those days, and it would almost be a collective discussion on the opposition and how to beat them. So in this respect, we can see the mass of information gathered on any specific opponent might be presented in a variety of ways to different groups.

Any watcher of Sky Sports will see how the technology has progressed, allowing images to be manipulated and organised so fluidly. This has been part of the continuing evolution of opposition scouting. However, down in non-league or youth-team football this technology and video may not be so readily available, and a presentation based on stats and analysis is much more likely and commonplace.

However the information is finally turned into a report, from whizzy broadcast quality image manipulation down to a set of PowerPoint slides, the basic content – the analysis itself – covers similar ground. There are a range of performance characteristics that will need to be considered, however the final report is going to be presented, and we will look at this content in the next sections.

The Research Phase

Before a game is even watched there is some work to be done, gathering background information on the opposition. This would include such things as:

- Performance in the season to date.
  Games played, results, points – general
  performance data.
- Context of the team. What are the websites
  and networks saying about the team – is it
  happy or unsettled, what have been the ins
  and outs of players recently?
- Which players are injured and unlikely to
  play. Are they significant?
- Who is suspended?
- Who is expected to return from injury
  or suspension?
- What is the general make-up of the squad –
  age range, experience?
- Who are the head coach and key staff?
  What is their track record, and how
  have they previously been known to have
  their teams play?

Depending on the level of the opposition and the
availability of data, the performance data for the season
so far could include a lot of useful stats – goals for
and against and where they have come from, different
performance at home or away, performance trends, etc.

The Analysis Phase

So now you will be looking at a range of games and
learning what you can about the team you are due to

play. Ideally, you will look at a range of games to give you a realistic and representative sample. If they are a team that adjusts to each opponent, you will need to watch a few games to see how this works out in practice. Similarly, if they play differently at home or away, or against teams with different general styles, then you can only learn that across a few suitable games. Ideally, you would watch three to five games for each upcoming opponent.

If you can access videos, this research and analysis phase can be done in a couple of days, presuming you are full-time and the production of the reports with the technological involvement as mentioned above is readily available to synchronise with this. Videos allow you to watch and rewatch, to capture every aspect that you wish of the play that is on view in the video. There is, of course, still a case that one or more live viewings would be very helpful to capture the team shape and movement that the video does not follow. However, it would be difficult to get that range of games in if you had to watch them all live, unless there were a team of scouts doing the opposition analysis. If you are only able to watch a team once or twice, then any subsequent analysis must include a caveat that it could be unrepresentative to varying extents.

There is a wide range of specialist notebooks and even digital plans to assist in the notetaking and information gathering that you will do, either live or on video. It is just a matter of trying different products until you find one that suits you – or even developing your own. If you are producing reports from live games then you will soon discover that there is a huge amount of information to be put together and noted, regardless of what medium you are using, be it old-fashioned notebooks, specialist scouting pads or digital products. Most people when they start to do this sort of reporting quickly comment that they did not realise how much is going on in any game! You will find your own way to systematically work through the info you want to capture.

Like any sort of scouting if you are watching live, it becomes a balancing act between closely observing the play and recording your impressions. I am sure we have all missed a key goal or pass from time to time! This again underlines the role that videos can play in helping you do a thorough job, even though, as I have mentioned, the cameras might miss something you want to capture. If the opposition goalkeeper tended to have a short starting position, for example, leaving them possibly more vulnerable to a ball over the top, then you might not see that on a video, depending on what happened in the game. If one defender tended to be slow at getting upfield when play moved that way, again you might not see that on video.

You will need some sort of plan – and the structured notebooks and digital products provide this to an extent. I will set out here the elements of an opposition team's performance that you will need to capture, one way or another. It is worth checking, if you intend to use a pre-printed notebook or system, whether they include all the aspects you feel are important to cover.

There is a range of opinions on this, and the different notebooks reflect this. You need to be happy that the list you use is as comprehensive as you need it to be, and you can exclude the things you do not feel are important. You must decide what your priorities are rather than fitting your report to a pre-set list of elements.

There follows an example of a set of key questions that you will need to answer in an opposition scouting report, organised into key sections:

Context
- How are they doing this season?
- What is their data on wins/losses/goals, etc?

Formations

- What formations do they use?
- Are they consistent, or when do they change?

As mentioned, coaches will adjust their formation to what their opposition may do, whereas others try to dictate play. Many coaches will have one formation for home games and may be more cautious when playing away. A 4-4-2 at home might become a 4-5-1 away, or a 3-4-3 at home might change to a 3-5-2 away. It may be more a matter of players not pushing forwards as much, or sitting a bit deeper; in other words, alterations within the same formation. Also, coaches may have 'go to' formations they use when chasing a game in the later stages, or closing a game out. It is normal for coaches to have worked on these options with their squads so they can apply them as needed. This underlines the need to watch several opposition games if possible to learn the range of formations that a squad uses. Formations can appear to be static when put down on a chart, yet they change and flow during a game. Hence we need to look at playing style.

Line-Ups

- What are their normal line-ups?
- Who plays where?

- Who is injured or suspended?

Playing Style – In Possession

- Do they play out from the back?
- Do they go long?
- How do they try to beat the press?
- Do they look to get the ball wide? If so, when and to whom?
- What is their instinct on their first pass – in defence, in midfield and up front?
- How do they react to attacking transition (i.e. when they win the ball)?
- Strengths and weaknesses?

The point here is to identify how they try to play – what is their game plan? Are they a team that likes to hit the channels from the back or do they play through the thirds? Are they looking to keep possession and, if so, what are the triggers to play forwards?

Playing Style – Out of Possession

- When and where do they press on defensive transition (i.e. when they lose the ball)?

Here we are looking for what their normal reaction is to losing the ball. Some teams will try to win the ball back straight away and press to do that, while others will tend to drop off and get their defensive shape back.

This may vary depending on the opposition or the state of the game.

- Do they defend in numbers and if so when?
- Strengths and weaknesses?

Set Plays – Defending

- How do they line up when defending corners?
- Are they alert and switched on to short corners?
- How effective is their aerial defending?
- When and how do they look to clear the ball?
- What are the key roles for them in defending corners and who performs them?
- What positions does the goalkeeper take up when defending corners?
- How do they deal with attacking free kicks?
- How effective are they at defending attacking free kicks within shooting distance?
- How useful is the goalkeeper at defending free kicks?
- Do they defend long throws well?
- Overall, do they favour zonal vs man-marking at set plays, or a mixture?

- Strengths and weaknesses in defending set plays?
- How does the goalkeeper deal with penalties?

Set Plays – Attacking

- Who takes their corners and free kicks?
- What type of corners do they use and when?
- What signals do they use for corners?
- What corner routines do they use?
- When a free kick is within shooting distance who takes it and what do they tend to do?
- What free kick routines do they use?
- Do they use long throws to attack? If so, who takes them and who is the usual target?
- Who takes their penalties and what is their pattern?

Goals Conceded

- How have they conceded goals?
- From where and when?

Goals Scored

- Where do their goals come from?
- What sort of moves and how are the goals scored?
- Who are their goal threats?

Key Players

- Who are their key players?
- What are their roles and significance?
- Who are their weak links and why?

It may well be that the head coach requires an individual assessment of each player (rather like the 'snapshots' we would do in a scouting report as explained in Chapter Five). So we are looking here for information on strengths and weaknesses – do they pass forwards, do they get caught in possession, are they quick, are they slow, what is their positional strength like, are they hot-headed, what is their stamina like, and so on.

Summary

- The overall match stats, covering goals for and against, possession, heat maps, stamina through games, usual formations and styles of play, strengths and weaknesses.

This is effectively an executive summary of the whole report, and the head coach may decide that this is enough information for their squad or some players within it. It consequently needs to present a concise but representative picture.

Appendix

- Summary of three to five games.

If the report is going to be more visual, in graphs or pictures or even video format, then this appendix might be where you log some of the basic underlying stats that are listed above for reference.

Opposition scouting is a specialist area within scouting. Many scouts will go through their entire career doing grassroots, academy or first-team scouting and never do any opposition scouting. As I mentioned at the top of the chapter it has more elements of coaching knowledge in it. Nevertheless, it is still based on observation and assessment, and these are generic scouting skills.

Consequently, there are different routes into opposition scouting. It may well be that the opposition scout worked with or for the head coach as a coach at some stage and they got to know each other in that context. There are other routes, however.

Famously, Andre Villas-Boas was living, as a 16-year-old, in the same apartment block as Bobby Robson when he was managing FC Porto. Villas-Boas, who has an English grandmother and speaks English well, got talking to Robson about football and was later appointed to Porto's technical department. Robson arranged for the precocious Portuguese to go on an FA coaching course and, in fact, Villas-Boas gained his 'UEFA C' licence at 17 and his 'UEFA B' licence at 18. Later in his career back at Porto, he worked for Jose Mourinho, who he followed to Chelsea and Inter Milan, where he was mostly undertaking opposition scouting. Villas-Boas later went on to manage Porto, Chelsea and Tottenham Hotspur among others.

This specialist scouting does not suit everyone, but it is an absorbing and important type of scouting. In my view all scouts should try compiling opposition scouting reports, maybe just using the pre-formatted report pads that I mentioned. It is a useful exercise and helps develop a scout's appreciation of the tactical aspects of the game.

Follow the QR code link to see me talking about opposition scouting:

Chapter Ten

Agents

THERE IS a war going on now in football. It is between FIFA and football agents. It has been born out of a crazy situation that football has allowed to happen by default over many years and it affects everyone in the game to one extent or another.

FIFA are again trying to regulate agents and set qualification standards. They are also seeking to stop agents representing more than one party in a transaction and, among other things, put a cap of 3 per cent on what an agent can earn from a transaction. Agents are up in arms and injunctions are flying about as I write this.

What is this all about? How does it affect scouts?

Years ago, agents were registered and licensed by FIFA. However, it became difficult to manage, so in practice was abandoned and became something of a free-for-all. Just about anyone could say they were an agent and be paid by clubs. Millions of pounds were flowing 'out of football' to agents from deals at the top end of the game.

It also became very messy. Sometimes agents were paid by all three parties in a transfer – the selling club, the buying club and, in theory, the player. This would be where a club had asked an agent to bring a deal together. In addition, in many of those cases, there were also other agents for the player involved who had to be paid too.

Hang on a minute, you say, surely the player pays his own agent out of what he gets? Just like entertainment agents, literary agents or even estate agents? Not always in football.

In his book on the business side of football, sports lawyer David Geey says: 'The beautiful game is a complicated business.'[12] That can certainly seem to be the case when we look at agents and their dealings. The majority of Premier League and top-end Football League transfers involve the buying club paying the agent, says Geey. So a club might engage an agent to help them find a player. Then there is the agent of the player in question, and there may be the agent of the

---

12 *Done Deal*, David Geey, Bloomsbury Sport, 2019.

buying club. All these agents will want paying if the deal comes off. It is often the buying club that picks up the tab and pays their own agent and maybe the player's agent too – or at least part of that commission, although there are then tax implications. However, as I have said, there are proposals afoot to change that, which will require players to pay their own agents and cap the fees at 3 per cent.

So how do you become a registered agent? There are two routes. If you were previously registered under the old FIFA schemes, there is a route for you whereby, if you have a clean record and so on, then you do not have to take the exam that has been created. However, if you are new to the game you must register to take an exam, which occurs about every six months. The exams comprise 20 multiple-choice questions and the pass mark is 75 per cent.

It costs around £500 to register as an agent. There are close to 2,000 registered agents operating in the Premier League and the English Football League. However, scouts will regularly be contacted by people who say they are representing this or that player, yet these people are not registered agents. It can become quite murky. If we are talking about young players, then these people will say, 'Well, they're too young to have agents. I'm just helping the family.' In some cases this may well be true but exactly how that works is not always clear.

So let's look at the legal situation. A player can sign up with an agent starting on 1 January in the year they turn 16 years of age. So, if their birthday is in September, say, they can sign up with an agent on 1 January that year, while they are still in their u15 season. This means you have the top u15 and u16 players who are much sought after, and agents will be circulating before that to get in with the families and be at the front of the queue. Consequently, agents will be looking at top u14s – and sometimes even younger – and positioning themselves to become their agents when it is legal to do so.

Given a player cannot earn money from the game until they are 17 and sign their first professional contract, why are agents so keen to get on board and what do they do to support the player and their family along the way? The work that agents do at this stage is really an investment in the future. They are looking to develop a strong relationship with the player in the hope that by the time they sign their second and third professional contracts they are beginning to get into good money. Obviously, this only applies to the very top talents.

In fact, the bigger agencies will often not take any commission until at least the second professional contract, and this may not be until the player is 18 or 19 years of age. So an agency could be investing four years of support, initially via the family, before there is any expectation of a return. Players can only sign for up to two years at a time with an agent, so agents are taking quite a risk with younger players. Clearly they must feel the potential return is worth it.

Let's assume that the second contract for a good young player at a Premier League club might be £20,000 pounds a week – just over £1m a year. An agent will typically charge 5 per cent or maybe 10 per cent, so they will get between £50,000 and £100,000 at that point. This is often paid as a lump sum up front, and, as we have seen, often paid by the club itself rather than the player! If that player goes on to become a top player, the next contract might be £250,000 a week, £13m a year. So that is a possible agent commission of between £650,000 and £1.3m per year – again, usually paid for by the signing club as a lump sum up front. It is those eye-watering amounts that fill the dreams of the would-be agents and drive years of investment in time and support. If you are supporting ten young players at 15 years of age, then you only need one to 'come good' in this way. In the meantime, you can see those huge sums on the horizon.

As the big new contracts may often be triggered by transfers or at least negotiations for a new contract, which may be sparked by interest from another club or media talk about that interest, you can see how agents can be viewed with suspicion by some club owners and sporting directors as they have an incentive to be disruptive.

Having said all that, clearly these sums are at the top end of the football world. For most football players we are not talking of anything like these scales of income. In the Premier League, the average income for a player is nearer £70,000 a week, just over £3.5m a year. In the Championship, it is more like £10,000 a week on average, which is over £500,000 a year. In League One you are looking at more like £5,000 a week, £250,000 a year, and in League Two it is much more like £2,000 a week, about £100,000 a year. These are all rough averages, and some players will earn a lot more and some a lot less. The point is that agents' fees will be between 5 and 10 per cent of these figures. So on average an agent might earn between £175,000 and £350,000 for a Premier League player's annual contract and between £25,000 and £50,000 for a Championship player. In League One the range is likely between £12,500 and £25,000 and in League Two around £5,000 to £10,000.

This gives us a rough idea of the scales of income and earnings we are talking about. An agent may bring other things to the table, particularly for the higher-profile players, such as product endorsements and advertising, and these can be big money-spinners too. However, again, as you go down the leagues they become less and less likely.

So what does an agent do? Martin Bewell was a good coach and manager in non-league football in the Midlands before becoming a national scout for Aston Villa for several years. He then moved into the agency world with Division X. 'As an intermediary, I guide them [the players] in all aspects of business, social and personal aspects of their lives,' Martin explained. 'This includes negotiating employment and endorsement deals for our players. We do a lot on their mentoring and development if they are a younger player. This is where I get most satisfaction as they know I only have their best interests at heart.'

Clearly, the negotiation of the contract is a major role for the agent. But let's look at young players who may not have reached that point. The agent's role is to look after every aspect of the player's football career, as we have heard, and this can involve advice on financial planning, social media activity and public relations, plus sponsorships such as boot deals, but also football development as well. The bigger agencies employ football coaches who will work one-on-one with their players, helping them develop their technique and game. They may have specialist movement or fitness coaches they can call upon too. Clearly, here there is potential overlap with what the player's club is doing. You would not want the player receiving contradictory advice on fitness regimes, for example. However, the smart agent will navigate through these potential conflicts.

The good agents will be in regular touch with their players and their families, attending games, and building a relationship of trust and support. As David Geey says: 'A football agent is rarely as glamorous a role as people imagine. It usually involves going to watch many, many football matches, and not all, if any, will be high-profile Premier League matches. For up-and-coming agents, the vast majority will be youth and academy matches as they try to build valuable connections with scouts, coaches, players, and their families (where permitted under the rules).'[13]

What makes a good agent? Martin Bewell has a clear picture of that:

> For me, it is your interaction with the player, being transparent and the agency you represent.

---

13 *Done Deal*, David Geey, Bloomsbury Sport, 2019.

I personally get to know the players that I look after. I am always available to discuss or chat with my players on any subject they call me to chat about. I would like to think from the skill set and life skills that I have gained over the years in football and life generally that I am able to give good information for them to digest and then make a decision or pathway that they decide to follow.

It does not suit everyone, though, and agents can have a bad reputation in some quarters of the game. Neil Sillett also had time as an agent:

I ran an agency myself after leaving Derby County and I really didn't enjoy being on that side of the game. I soon understood why, as it's a game for the fearless and the game where as an agent you are seen as one of a group who lack scruples or morals, which never sat well with me. Having said all that, when working in a club environment the agents are a vital part of a scout's network. They can get to connections that the scout isn't able to, due to the regulations and the way the recruitment processes work.

Now mainly working as an international-level scout for Scotland, Neil has kept in touch with some agents. He added, 'So, although they aren't quite so important when working at international levels, I have kept in contact with quite a few. I often speak with a handful of reputable guys who try and do the right things by their players.'

You can see that along this path there are many points where an agent will want to lean on a scout for information. At the very beginning, when the agent is trying to identify potential talent, the network of contacts they have built up with key scouts is vital. The agent will be out looking for new talent, and the bigger agencies employ people to do just this – their own talent scouts in effect. Consequently, it is a normal part of a scout's working life to be contacted by agents that they know and to be asked about players: 'Have you heard about player X at club Y? Heard he's doing well.'

If you work as a scout, particularly in academy or first-team scouting, then you can expect regular calls of this type from agents. This can, of course, work to your advantage. You can get to know who is playing well or looking for a move. This informal exchange of information can be vital and helpful. However, you must be cautious. You will need to learn which agents you can trust to keep information confidential, and which will cause you a problem. If an agent calls and says, 'I hear your player Y is going to be released at the end of the season,' and you say, 'Yes, I think he will be,' then the last thing you want is for the next call you receive to be from your head of recruitment saying, 'What the hell is going on? I've just had the parent of player Y on the phone, who says his agent has told him you said he was being released.'

What can also be difficult is when you have a player approaching that time when they are going to sign to an agency and there are two or more agents vying for their business. Agents may contact you seeking confirmation of some interest so they can feed this back to the parents and show they are in touch with clubs who are interested in their son to get an edge in the competition.

You will also be contacted by people who say they are agents or suggest they are and try to pitch a player to you. Again, of course, this can be very useful and a source of potential new players to have a look at. However, I have to say that you do have a lot of time wasted with so-called agents pitching you players that are nowhere near the level you want. I had yet another 'agent' recently trying to convince me that their 22-year-old centre-back playing in lower leagues in France was right for the Premier League. I kept explaining that I did not deal with international scouting, but, anyway, at that age a player must be potentially a first-team player and is that at all realistic coming from that level? When has it ever happened before?

The overseas issue is another constant time-wasting problem. People purporting to be agents pitch you players who have no chance of getting the required FIFA points to be eligible for international clearance. They might be under 18 years of age and, while clubs can apply for exemptions, it is very difficult to bring players in, including from countries within the European Union who we could have previously signed (before Brexit) at 16 years of age. Yet these agents do not seem to know how the FIFA process works for players transferring from one country to another. This does beg the question of what sort of agents are they? Also, when I explain to these 'agents' that I do not deal with international transfers, they often ask, 'Who does at your club?' Again it makes me wonder what sort of agents they are, because surely an agent worth their salt would know who is who at a big Premier League club?

For all that, as a scout, of course, you never know whether this player they are talking about could be a good one. So the normal urge of a scout is to check out every player that is thrown at them, and that is a good and healthy impulse. It may be a case of passing the info along to whoever deals with that age and area within your club. However, you can waste a lot of time along the way.

But let's be clear. Many people in the game find it easy to criticise agents and hold them responsible for all the ills of the modern money-ridden game. At times it seems that agents are down there with estate agents, tax inspectors and traffic wardens as the least popular occupations! I must say the criticism makes me feel a bit uncomfortable. Clubs use agents and, in fact, scouts use agents. So it is a bit hypocritical to bemoan the agents' role across the board. There are many agents – in big and small agencies – that really do a good job in helping their clients develop and get the best from their invariably short careers, and I have absolutely no issue with that at all. If a player gets to the end of a contract or is released, then the agent who finds them a suitable club is doing a great service and deserves to be paid for it.

I asked the top scout Conner Agar what connections he has with agents: 'Good ones. It's like anything, there are good and bad, and some do it for financial benefits and yet some are a guiding light for young professionals. I've been very lucky to build good connections with good agents and they can be so useful in your network.'

There are understandable restrictions on clubs directly approaching players and parents, as we have discussed earlier. If a club or a scout wants to know how a player is doing and whether they might be interested in a move or whatever, then, obviously, if you know their agent it is an easy call to make. As I have mentioned, scouts can benefit from the information that an agent shares. Again it is all a matter of knowing who you can trust.

I know a lot of scouts who have gone to work for agencies. It seems to suit some and not others, but it is a route into agency work if that is where you want to go. A lot of the network and contacts are the same for either role, and there is a lot of overlap. I have spent many a cold, wet evening watching a game where virtually all the other few bedraggled spectators are scouts or agents.

I asked Martin Bewell what the difference, in his experience, is between being a scout and an agent, as he has performed both roles:

> If I am honest, it's night and day. As the scout you identify talent (i.e. the player), and make sure all the relevant paperwork is completed for him to attend at the academy, and then hand them over to the coaches at the football club on their first introduction night. As an

intermediary, you are more connected with the player and the player's family and friends, which is something I thoroughly enjoy.

Whatever happens with the current dispute with FIFA, agents are part of the landscape of football and, as a scout, you will come across them. They might even be seeking you out. Either way, if you choose wisely they can be a key part of your network.

Here's a link to a cautionary tale about agents:

Chapter Eleven

Parents

WHEN WE started doing the little social media videos to build up a profile for this book, the overwhelming majority of questions came from parents. They wanted to know how scouting worked. They wanted to know how their child could get scouted, what happens when they are and what they could do to help along the way. There were a lot of practical questions about ages you can sign and distances and so on. Bread-and-butter stuff for scouts but, of course, parents may well be new to this world of academy football and just did not know what to expect and how it worked. We tried to help with the videos, and I want to help further in this chapter.

One whole set of questions related to what scouts look for, and I have covered that earlier in the book. I have also made clear that the Code of Conduct for

Scouts requires the first point of contact for a scout at a grassroots game to be the team manager and not the parents. So, for many parents, the first contact they will have from a scout would be the team manager or coach calling them over and introducing them to the scout. It may be the case that the whispers have whipped along the touchlines and parents are saying, 'See that bloke there, he's a scout.'

Many times I have been at a tournament, for example, and had a kid come up to me and ask, 'Are you a spotter?' It may be that the club coat is a big giveaway! In fact, one northern club did not really engage scouts on a proper contracted basis but issued them with club coats and sent them out without any further identification, hence these were often disparagingly referred to as 'coats not scouts' by 'proper scouts'.

Some scouts prefer not to be in club kit so they can be 'incognito'. My own view is that from the clubs' point of view, it's good to have their people in club kit, showing they are interested in local football and active. It looks professional – or should do! It's good public relations.

The scout should show you their accreditation. This should be up-to-date photo ID issued by their club. This is important from a safeguarding point of view, let alone the professionalism of the scout. They should be able to give you (and the team manager) a business card with their contact details on it. I say 'should' because we know in practice many clubs, particularly smaller clubs, may not provide scouts with kit or even business cards. There should be photo ID though, as a bare minimum. So, if you are a parent and are approached by someone saying they are a scout but they do not have any real ID, then I think you are entitled to be sceptical and cautious.

But let's assume they have identification. They will probably ask you about your child. How long they have been playing? Do they play anywhere else? Have they been in an academy? And so on. The conclusion of the chat might be that they take your contact details and say they will watch your child again. That is fine, they are just gathering information at this stage. However, it may be that they invite you into something. It is important that you clarify exactly what they are asking you into. Is it a full academy trial? Is it a trial game or a training session? Is it with a 'development group' or community programme?

In the past, it was possible to bring in a player for one or two training sessions with their academy age group to see how they did. Strictly speaking, this is not allowed now. You cannot have an unsigned player coming in and training with an academy group. They must be on proper academy trial forms. However, some smaller clubs still do this and seem to get away with it. It may be that the club has 'development groups' or filtering processes of one sort or another. These used to be called 'shadow squads', although 'development groups' is a more common term nowadays. Basically, these are groups of unsigned players who one way or another are being assessed as to whether they are ready for an academy trial. A club may have a whole range of these groups across the ages. However, one criticism of these has been that in some clubs they are, in practice, just places to 'park' players and that these players can be kept there in this holding process for months and even a whole season.

They are unsigned and can still play for their local grassroots clubs, so all is not lost. Maybe you will feel that they are getting some extra training and that is worth it. I think the key thing here for parents is to clarify with the scout just what the sessions are. If they are a development group or filtering process, then how long do players normally attend them? How does the decision-making process work?

Sometimes a scout may be referring the player to the club's community scheme. Again, that is fine, as there are some very good programmes and they can be a good pathway into an academy. But be aware that they are often paid-for sessions. Academy trials – and development groups – should be free, but community programmes often are on a 'pay for play' basis.

So, okay, let's assume the scout has asked you to bring the child into a formal academy trial. There are academy trial forms to be signed for either the Premier League or the English Football League, and many clubs send those to parents electronically so they can be processed via the 'docu-sign' system online. You will need to send a copy of the player's passport, a head-and-shoulders photo – a phone photo is fine – and proof of address by way of a utility bill within the last three months. This is all part of the process of proving where the child lives, what their nationality status is, etc. You need to get all this completed and returned to the club and they then have to register the player with the relevant league before they can start training with the academy squad, let alone playing.

There are distance restrictions on who can register for a trial – or sign for an academy. The basic rule of thumb is that if a player cannot sign, then they cannot trial. The player must live within an hour's drive of the training ground if they are between u9 and u11, then one and a half hours from u12 to u16. Then it is more lenient for the older players. The basis of this is not to have children travelling too far on school nights to get to and from training. Hence, the location of residence must be proved in some ways to check the player qualifies.

There is an exception to this for Category 1 academies. If such an academy can offer full-time education, they can sign a player from the age of 14 upwards, as I have mentioned elsewhere. However, there are not many clubs that would want to move a child at that young age. It does happen later, though, that a club, maybe from another part of England, will want to bring a child into their full-time education to get them signed at a younger age rather than wait for them to reach 16 and be eligible for signing as a scholar. If they are a Category 1 academy, they can do this from the age of 14 upwards. Perhaps it is more common, though, that where this does happen it is usually more likely from age 16 upwards.

If an academy offers full-time education, and only the biggest academies really can, then they must be able to honour this for four years. What this means is that even if the academy decides to release the player, they must honour the education commitment for this four-year period. Of course, it may be the case that in such circumstances the club and the family agree to part ways and the player may change schools.

However, this makes it clear that such an offer of full-time education is a big commitment for the club and therefore would only be done in quite exceptional circumstances, and obviously only for players the club really believes in.

So, if a player is under 14 and they are being offered full-time education, this means their four years will take them through into the scholar years of u16 to u18. This means they should in effect be being offered a scholarship. Furthermore, it will take them past their 17th birthday, so the issue of that first professional contract comes into consideration as well. You can see that such an offer is, therefore, a major commitment from a club to a player and would not be given lightly, nor would it be considered as anything less than a major significant life step for the player and the family.

Okay, let's assume the scout is inviting the player into a full academy trial. What does this entail?

The player will sign trialist forms and for the period of the trial will be just the same as a signed player. The length of a trial is up to eight weeks. This can be extended by a further four weeks if the club applies before the last week of the trial and the parents sign the necessary form.

The trialist will train with the academy squad and be eligible to play in all the games. It must be said that not all academies will guarantee the trialists the same playing time as the signed players. Others will share the normal game time but retain the right to pick the best possible team for cup tournaments, etc., which may exclude the trialist. From a scout's point of view, and I am sure for many parents in this position, this is extremely frustrating as you want to see the trialist show what they can do.

The trialist and parents will be invited in to the first training session. I have always felt that the scout should be there for this first session at least. It is important that there is one friendly face among the many new people the trialist and family will be meeting, to welcome the player to the club. It is good practice for the scout to be there to assist and show them around. The better academies will do a proper induction presentation for the trialist and family, explaining just what they can expect over the length of the trial and, crucially, explaining how and when decisions will be made and conveyed.

I think the scout should help prepare the trialist and the parents for the experience of being on trial. We must understand that for a young person to walk into a dressing room of unfamiliar faces, many of whom have been together for years, is a very difficult thing. In one sense a trialist is, of course, looking to take someone's shirt. It is the same as any new player coming into a club at any level. It is a competitive sport and if we are talking about academies then it is an elite sport environment. It can be a challenging environment for trialists to come into and will not suit everyone.

I always point out to trialists and their families that it is quite understandable that they may get to the point where they feel, 'Well, this is okay, I'm as good as anybody else in this squad.' That is an understandable human reaction and benchmark that they may seek to attain. However, in most cases this will not be enough. To be signed, a player must show they are better than others. I think it is important that the scout helps the parents understand that this is the level of performance that must be achieved. Personally, I take the view that in most cases it is not worth adding a player to a squad if they are just one of the average players. There must be something that they bring to the party. It may be that in terms of their performance level they are average, but they have high potential. Either way, it should be made clear to parents and the players at the beginning of the trial exactly what is expected of them and what they must do to get signed. A trial can be a very stressful experience for the player and the family, and it is of course in everybody's interest if the club can help settle the player into the group and help find a way that they could show the best that they can offer.

Having said that, some clubs do it well. They are careful and considerate about integrating trialists into the squad, and the astute coach can go a long way to make this engagement easier. Some coaches ask one of the established players to be a 'buddy' and do the introductions. Other academies talk with their players about making people welcome and so on.

The scout needs to be aware of these issues and can act as a go-between for the parents and the academy if needed. They can help smooth out any difficulties. I always think the scout should watch the player in training and at least one game. This not only provides some continuity for the family, but it also helps the scout gauge the level of the trialist vis-à-vis the academy squad.

Once the trial is underway it is always helpful if the scout can keep in touch with the family and ideally gets the opportunity to come along and see the player in a game. From the scout's point of view, this helps you come to an understanding of how the child is doing in practice and whether they are showing their full abilities. It helps you to see them in the context of the actual age group in a real game. You may be able to help the club by providing some feedback to the family and the player as the trial progresses, but it is important that this is always done in conjunction with the academy recruitment team to make sure there is a consistent level of response and to minimise the danger of mixed messages.

As a trial comes to an end there will be some sort of decision meeting, usually in the academy. This would be where the opinions of the coaches who have worked with the player, plus perhaps the strength and conditioning people and sports scientists who tested the player, and the scouts who have seen the player, will all have a chance through one means or another to give their opinions as to what should happen with this player. Having said that, what I have just described is probably best thought of as good practice, whereas I know that in a lot of academies it is not as structured as that.

It has always seemed strange to me that some academies will have scouts out every week doing reports on players from other clubs that they might think about trying to sign, yet not so many have scouts doing reports on players who are already on trial with them. I think that surely these players should be assessed in the same way by the same criteria as a player who you may be able to sign from another academy or you may not. Yet, in practice, a lot of academies do not do this thoroughly. Decisions can sometimes be made by just one person. This may be the academy recruitment manager, the academy manager or a head coach of some sort, depending on the structure of the club. Again, it seems strange to me that there is not always a consistent and comprehensive consideration of the range of views of the people who have worked with or watched the trialist when it comes to making the decision on whether to sign them. The better-organised academies will do this in a formal way and log their decisions, and I am sure this contributes in time to a better understanding of their own recruitment practices and gives them the data to reflect on recruitment decisions when looking back at the end of the season.

In my experience it is not normally the case that the original scout will be involved in this final decision. This may be because the decision-making process at the academy excludes the scout. It may be thought that the original scout could be biased in favour of 'their player'. I do understand this point of view and I have seen over the years some scouts, including some very experienced and successful scouts, who just do not seem to understand that their players will not always be signed. There are, of course, good scouts who can see the broader picture and who can contribute to an objective discussion on the merits and weaknesses of a particular player in relation to the age-group squad.

Overall, I do understand why many academies do not include the original scout in these decision meetings. However, I do feel it is very important that the scout is informed of the decision and whether the parents yet know that decision, so they can get involved in the end game, whatever that might be. For example, if we are looking at a situation where a player is not going to be signed, then the scout should know that this is going to happen and when. The academy will undertake this difficult meeting by whatever their normal process is, and then the scout can be involved in supporting the family in whatever the next steps might be.

This might seem strange to some scouts. They may think that their job is to bring the players in and from then on it is up to the academy to manage the trial process and its aftermath. I disagree. If the scout is the first contact of a club with the parents and player, I think they should be part of the process at the end of the trial. I happen to take the view that the club has a responsibility to look beyond the conclusion of the trial. I think they should be able to help the player reintegrate back into grassroots by making sure their scout continues to monitor them and has contact with them. They would then show through that action that the club is not just washing their hands of a discarded player.

If it is the case that the family and player would like to go to another club for a further trial, then I believe it is part of the role of the academy and the scout involved to facilitate this connection. Let me be clear about what I mean here. I think if an academy has taken a player on a formal trial but then decided to release them, it is important that they continue to show consideration and care. This would show in the way that the decision is conveyed to the family and player, which I will come on to, but also in terms of monitoring the player into the future and helping connections to be made with other academies if required.

If the family of the young player, after being told that they are not going to be signed, says that they would like to be put in contact with other academies, then I think the scout may well be the person who makes that connection. Again, it comes down to the scout's network, but potentially here a scout is doing a favour to another club and, of course, helping the family and the player in question, which can be very useful in the future. It is very important that any such connections are made with the full understanding and blessing of the academy recruitment team but there should be no objection to another club being alerted to a player's availability once the first club has made a decision not to sign them. In most cases, scouts and academies will want the players to do well for them to go on to achieve their potential.

As I am writing this, I recall that just recently the parents of a player we had on trial a few months ago phoned me to say thank you because the club I had referred them to after we released the player had just signed them. I was very pleased for the player and the family and felt that I had done my job properly. In fact, the club in question had contacted me the day before to say that they were going to sign the player and thanked me for referring the player to them. So not only had I done my job and helped the player and their family in a responsible way but now I have another local club that perhaps might feel they owe me a favour. This could play out in all sorts of ways in the future. It may be that we become interested in one of their players and I can assist in finding out through the academy some background on that player. There are several ways in which clubs can work together and, as ever in life, sometimes you must give a bit to get a bit!

Let's now look at the ways in which the decision on a trial is relayed to the player and the family. Again, let's focus at this point on a release. So, the player has been in for eight or even 12 weeks and it now has come to that decision point. Internally, a decision-making meeting has been held, or the decision has been reached by whichever means the academy applies. Now that decision must be relayed to the player and their family. It is not usual for the original scout to be involved in the communication of this final decision, but it does happen, and it can be useful. I have no problem in involving the original scout, which for good or bad has been a key part of my job.

There are different views on whether the players should be in this meeting when they are going to be released. The way I approach it for the younger players, let's say from u9 to u12, is that I will tell the parents the decision and then offer to meet with the player and the parents together to tell the player myself face to face, if that is what the parents want. They know their child best, so I give them the option of whether they want to break the news to the player themselves or have me do it. I must say, in most cases the parents will ask me to tell the player myself.

For the older players from u13 upwards I would normally arrange to have the player in with the parents when I convey the unhappy news. I take the view that at those ages they need to be there first-hand and should be old enough to understand the process. There is no easy way to convey this bad news. However you dress it up, there is a big 'no' in the middle of this conversation. Some parents and players only really hear the 'no', and I can understand that. When I read sometimes of parents who seem quite bitter and disenchanted with the academy world, it can often be traced back to at some stage them and their child hearing that 'no'.

I think every recruitment person who has had to perform this task of saying no to a player and their family at the end of a trial will have their own way of doing it. It is something that I continually review in my own mind as to whether I am doing it as well as I could or how it could be improved. My view is that it is important to be honest, and this applies throughout the trial process. It is important to give some reasonable feedback on a player in terms of their performance while on trial and to explain the basis of the decision. This may sound obvious, but you do hear from parents that when they had this meeting and were told 'no', then that was it. It was the first feedback they received. I am not sure this is always the case, given that it is perhaps human nature to be focused on whether there is going to be a 'yes' or a 'no', and everything else might be a bit of a blur. I can only do my best in these circumstances, as everybody no doubt tries to do.

I try to explain how the decision was made, who made it and what the strengths and the weaknesses of the player have been perceived to be. I will then talk about the overall squad and how we thought the player may or may not fit in. This may include mentioning that there are players in the age group below in that position and we did not want to block them, if that is the case. Whatever the circumstances, I will try to give a clear, concise but honest assessment of how the decision was made and why. We can then talk about the next steps, and this is where the monitoring by the original scout or the referral to another club comes in. I always say to parents that they may want to think about this for a couple of days and come back to me, thereby making it clear that I am not bringing down the guillotine on our contact with the family in any way and that we will continue to help. This seems to me to be just common courtesy. It is also, in my opinion, the proper and professional way to approach these difficult decisions.

We are dealing with elite sports. In elite sports there is selection. Where there is selection there is rejection. This is just how it is, and if you do not want your child to go through this process, then do not put them into elite sports. Having said that, it is then our responsibility in the academies to make sure the decision-making process is as careful and considerate as it can be.

If the decision is to sign the player, then of course the whole atmosphere and context is very different. I think the original scout should very much be involved in the signing process, and if there are photos to be taken then that scout deserves to be alongside the player they have brought into the club. This is an easy and obvious type of recognition of the role of the scout and of their achievements. But it is again surprising how often this is overlooked by clubs. The better practice is for the original scout to be involved.

From the parents' point of view the signing will be literally a signing of forms by them and the player to register their child as a signed player with the proper authorities. There are usually some monitoring forms as well. The length of time a player is signing for will vary according to their age. Up to u12 the normal practice is that it is a year-by-year, or should I say season-by-season registration. So, for example, if a player signs in December of their u12 year, that registration will normally last through to the end of the following June in that u12 year. From u13 upwards there are usually two-year registrations. Players will therefore sign for their u13 and u14 years. Then they will sign for their u15 and u16 years as another two-year registration. And then, of course, we are into the scholar ages.

It is possible for players to leave in the middle of a registration, but the club must at least honour the registration from their point of view. It is important that scouts and parents understand the commitments that clubs are making when a player is presented to them. It is important that it is clearly understood when that registration will next be up for the retain and release process. This is something that a good academy will explain to parents and, of course, an experienced scout will know this context and be able to help convey it to the parents.

As a scout, I am asked how parents can help their child progress in football. It is a commonplace argument and discussion among academy coaches and scouts that parents can sometimes hinder rather than help. However, let's look at the positive side first. I think a parent needs to be realistic about their child, which is easier said than done if you do not have a lot of experience of the football world or the standards within it. Most parents do not know the step up in level between a grassroots team and an academy. They may never have seen academy football at all or have no experience or contact with it. This is all quite understandable, but again it is an area where a good scout can help by painting the pictures as clearly as possible.

We want our children to enjoy sports, particularly team sports because they teach so many lessons about life. No one wins unless we all win. Kids can meet all sorts of other kids their own age but maybe from different backgrounds, and the whole experience of playing sports at a local level can be great fun and a great way to make friends. It is also a very healthy pastime, of course. For many parents, the fact that it is a way of getting their children away from one screen or another is in itself a major positive. Then parents may start getting ideas that their child can go further, and they maybe have the ambition to help their child get access to professional football through an academy. This is all quite understandable and natural and can be a very positive process.

It is true that sometimes some parents are living out their own dreams in terms of football progression or some sort of local celebrity and fame by their child being successful at a professional club. To be honest, I have no problem with that. Parents have a range of motivations and are entitled to their own opinions and aspirations. From a scout's point of view, it is important to get a picture of what the parents are interested in, what they want for their child and how much they understand about the process that they may be about to enter.

Parents can help by encouraging their children and getting them to the games and training. This can be a major commitment and a major difficulty in families where perhaps there is more than one child or where money is tight and it is difficult to transport children around. It is important as scouts that we never underestimate the commitment required of families where their children are edging their way into academy football, which is very demanding. Most academy groups will train three or four times a week and have a game too, so someone has to get the children to these training sessions and games, and it is invariably their families that pick this up. The scouts must appreciate that and also make the parents aware that it is part of the package. Beyond that, parents can help by being positive and encouraging their children, without going over the top.

Unfortunately, any scout will tell you stories of parents who perhaps get carried away, and we have all sadly seen instances of conflict and even fighting between parents on the touchline of children's games. This is crazy, and regardless of the football process it is just not the way to behave and not good for our children. I understand as much as anybody the passions that are involved in football and the strength of the desire to win. I acknowledge that, as a parent myself, I have not always been the most easy-going on a touchline. However, there is a right and wrong way to express yourself and parents need to bear this in mind. I do not want to take the passion out of the game at all, but we have to exercise judgement here.

I mentioned earlier watching a u10 player in a grassroots game for the second time. I had seen him play before, but this was a cup final. His team lost, and when I went to speak to his dad and the child after the game the boy was in tears. The dad said, 'Oh I'm sorry, he's so upset.' I said, 'No, that's no problem, he's just lost a cup final! He's entitled to be upset.' Of course, if he had burst into tears on the pitch during the game that might not have been such an easy one to understand or accept. Even then, when we are looking at kids as young as six and seven at the very start of their football journeys, then we do need to remember that they are very young children. If a player of 16 is struggling to control his emotions during a game, that is more of an issue or concern.

But it should matter to all of them. Winning does matter, but parents can help keep everything in context and perspective. They can be positive and encouraging. They can demonstrate good sportsmanship and a good attitude to winning and losing. I have always taken the view with my children that it is important that they learn to be good sports, but I would never expect to teach them to be good losers.

Again, as a scout, we may be asked by parents how they can help their child deal with the nerves that might come with playing in an important game when they are being watched or even when they come in for a trial game or a trial itself. This is difficult because we do not know the child in most cases, so advice can only be quite generic. Over the years I have found that what can mostly help a young player is for parents to encourage them to focus on the process, in other words the immediate actions of the game in front of them, and not to focus on any possible outcome, such as getting a trial or being signed. Parents can help in this regard by choosing what they talk about to the player before the game.

If your conversation is about their game and is quite normal, then encouraging their confidence in this way is, in my opinion, more likely to be helpful than saying such things as 'remember, this is a big game', 'you really need to do well today', 'you can get a trial if you play well today', and so on. That would just build the pressure, and unless that is what you want to do, then be careful.

Focusing on the process and the immediate action can help take away some of the anxiety and some of the pressure. If a player makes a mistake, as every player will, then it is important that they try to simplify their game and not try to overreach in response. For example, if a player misplaces a 20-metre pass, you see them sometimes trying a 30-metre pass straight away to recoup their confidence. In most cases I think that is not advisable. I would tell any player in such circumstances to shorten their game and get some five- and ten-metre passes going, get some success and build their confidence before letting the 'Hollywood passes' flow. It might be worth pointing out in such circumstances that generally scouts are more impressed by somebody who does the simple things well and consistently rather than occasionally pulling off a fancy trick but giving the ball away more often than not.

Dealing with nerves is difficult for some players but not for others, who seem to have no nerves at all. What we must say, though, is that if a player is going to make progress in the professional game, then they are going to encounter bigger and bigger games and more difficult circumstances, so dealing with the pressure that comes with that is part of becoming a professional footballer. While we do not expect a child of ten to show a mature, experienced, professional attitude, we do need parents to understand that they will need to learn how to deal with nerves. It is important that they understand that becoming nervous is not a problem. We can help children learn to use their nervous energy and to focus it on their game and their physical effort. What we cannot do is pretend to them that there is no reason to be nervous when their mind and maybe even our words are telling them the exact opposite. It is a process of dealing with nerves, not denying them.

There are other ways in which parents may feel they can help their child develop. There is a growing field of 1-2-1 coaching now, with many coaches offering such support throughout the country. For goalkeepers I would say this is vital if it can be arranged, as the technical development of goalkeeping skills is not something that most general run-of-the-mill coaches can provide. Particularly as a player gets older, these goalkeeping technical skills become more of an issue when they try out for an academy. They may be up against other goalkeepers who have had this sort of technical support and specialist training since they were six or seven years old within an academy setting, and it is very difficult to compete if you have not had that input.

With all extra coaching, though, there is the issue of cost, and some of the 1-2-1 coaching is very expensive and beyond the means of many families. It also must be said that not all coaches are good 1-2-1 coaches. In my opinion, it is a specialist type of coaching, and if you are thinking of getting your child 1-2-1 coaching and have the means to provide it, I strongly suggest that you shop around. It is worth listening to other parents' views on who has improved the individual skill of a player as opposed to just giving them some drills to do. Having said that, there are some top 1-2-1 coaches who really do help players develop and, as we saw in the chapter on agents, there are some agencies that provide this sort of 1-2-1 coaching as part of their services. So, I would say overall that, yes, it is something to explore if you can afford it, but be cautious. It is not essential, however.

We can now look at what parents may experience once they are in an academy. I was passing the treatment room a while ago when I saw one of our signed players who had come through my trialist programme a year before. He was getting some plasters put on his feet. I asked him what the problem was and he said he had some blisters from new boots. I noticed that the boots he was wearing were not our club-issue boots but another brand. I found out later that this lad, who has only recently signed for an academy at u13, already had a boot deal from another manufacturer. It just goes to show the amount of interest there is from sports kit manufacturers in academy players. Parents need to be ready for these approaches. For most players, a boot deal would just involve regularly providing boots, but given that these can cost well over £100 a pair, it is not something that most families would turn away. To be honest, I see no problem with this in general terms as long as it is kept in perspective, but I would advise parents to keep the club aware of any commercial approaches.

Then will come approaches from agents as players get older, and I have already mentioned that I think the way to deal with this is to get advice from other parents when it comes to picking an agent. It may be as the scout that you are asked by a parent which agency they should go to or sign with. You must be careful here because clubs cannot really seem to be favouring one agency over another. That would seem to me to be a bit of a conflict of interest, so a scout needs to be cautious. But I do think it is important that parents talk to other parents about this and find out who is with which agency, who is treated well, what sort of support they get and what they can expect.

As a scout I think we have a responsibility to parents to support them through the whole process of their contact with the club and beyond. It is worth remembering, as the parents can be very useful to you in a whole number of ways. This, of course, applies not just to those players who you bring in for a trial or some sort of further action within an academy but also to parents who you meet along the way as a scout. If you are professional, polite and helpful, then word will get around. If you become known as a scout who is a good person and helpful, it will help you grow your network and, as I have mentioned so many times, the scout's network is their key to progress and success.

It can be difficult for parents to get an honest assessment of their child, so they know where they are in terms of academy standard and what they need to work on. Some academy scouts and coaches seem reluctant to give this type of detailed feedback. This came up so often in comments from parents on our social media feeds that we decided to set up a business offering professional independent scouting assessments of players.[14]

---

14 www.thescoutinggame.co.uk

For parents, I would say that we all need to remember this is sport and it is supposed to be enjoyable. But one of the reasons it is enjoyable is because of the passions involved. It is difficult not to get carried away at times with progress into a professional game and all that it entails. Scouts can help you, and a good scout is a key contact for you as a parent just as much as you are for them.

Do parents help or hinder? Follow the QR link to hear my response to that question:

Chapter Twelve

Scouts and Bias

I AM biased. So are you. We all have biases. There are some we are aware of and some that we are not. They come from our mental processes or maybe from our personal life experiences or the culture we live in.

As scouts, we should be aware of our biases or at least be on the lookout for them as they can affect every decision we make. We often hear that 'football is about opinions'. What about if all your opinions are skewed before you start, influencing you to like certain types of players in certain circumstances?

I have noticed over the years that as a scout I do tend to look more favourably on certain types of players. It is something that I have discussed with other scouts. In fact, in conversation recently a fellow scout, when talking to me about a certain player he had seen, said, 'You'd love him, he's your sort of player.' This made me think! I am trying to be at least conscious of my biases.

We discussed what he meant, and it became apparent that he had noticed a pattern where I favoured those players who demonstrated great drive and a will to win. I think this is fair enough. I do know other scouts who I would characterise as preferring small, skilful players, for example, or those who are always drawn to pace. Another very experienced scout I know always looks favourably on left-footed players as he feels they can be in demand later in their careers.

It does seem that certain academies may favour certain types of players from time to time. They might have a lot of technical players or maybe more big strong physical types. This may reflect the types of players they have around them in their catchment areas or reflect the types of players they think will succeed at their academy and go on to their first team. However, it may be that the key decision-makers in that academy's recruitment set-up favour certain types of players. I receive many comments from parents saying something like 'academies are only interested in the big strong athletes', when their child may be smaller and more technical. However, conversely, I do also have comments from parents saying, 'They only want the little dribblers, not the more athletic types.' There may well be some sour grapes mixed in there but, having said that, it does appear that certain academies favour certain types of players.

Earlier in the book I mentioned how important it is to try to get a variety of scouts to view a player if possible, because after a few views most of us become quite set on our decisions and just repeat them. This is called 'confirmation bias'. It is related to the way our brains work. Because we have so much information around us and besieging us in everyday life, our brains tend to make patterns and create expectations of what will come along next. This is 'predictive processing'. What is more, the brain may then just discount information that we come across that contradicts the assumption we have made, and even ignore this other new information. This leads us to the 'confirmation bias', where the brain focuses on info that supports current beliefs.

In scouting, we can see this play out so often. We watch a player, we decide on them, and we then in practice only seek confirmation from further information we get that supports our original decision. 'You see,' we might say, 'I told you he was quick,' when we see something that confirms our original opinion, and we may not bother to review the new context of a slower game or whatever. Our brain is making shortcuts for us. This is a subconscious process. We do not decide to do it. It just happens naturally. We can, however, at least be aware of when it might be happening.

There are other biases we should be aware of. There is 'survivor bias', where we look at someone who has succeeded and then investigate their pathway and assume this is the correct pathway for others who want to succeed. For example, we might look at Jude Bellingham, now recognised as one of the best young midfield players in the world. We may note that he started his football journey at Birmingham City, coming up through their academy and making his first-team debut with them at the age of 16. (This was away in the EFL Cup at Portsmouth. I was at that game. In fact, I was there to report on Jude Bellingham – he was already on the big clubs' radar. Funnily enough, his dad, Mark, had played for me when I was manager at Cheltenham Town.) As we know, Jude went on to Borussia Dortmund, then a couple of years later he joined Real Madrid for a base fee of €103m with the potential to rise to over €133m with add-ons.

'Survivor bias' might lead us to conclude that if it worked for Jude it can work for others, so maybe joining a relatively smaller club and getting into their first team at a young age is the way to go. It leads us to sort of reverse engineer the pathway and perhaps leads us to generalise about the pathway because it worked out for Jude. It disregards the many other players who make it to the top by joining the big academies (examples from Jude's England contemporaries would be Phil Foden, Marcus Rashford, Reece James). Nor does it consider all the many young players who also went to Birmingham City's academy and have not ended up at Real Madrid!

Another bias is 'anchoring bias', which is an over-reliance on the first piece of information we receive. This is extremely common in scouting. I know one very senior recruitment head who is notorious for making up his mind about players based on immediate impressions of a few minutes. He might be saying 'no, he's rubbish' or 'yes, sign him', but you will know straight away. To be honest, there is a bit of playing to the crowd in this case and it might be excused as a purposefully provocative act to get responses from other scouts. However, I do think there is also an element of genuine bias at play there too.

As scouts, we do have to make our minds up about players. No one appreciates those scouts who always sit on the fence and do not conclude 'yes, we should sign him' or 'no, we should not'. Sometimes we must make our decisions more quickly than we would like, as we simply do not have time for successive views on a player. We might know they are just about to sign for another club, for example, so we have to make our minds up now.

We should seek a balanced approach, in my view. Of course, we will gain initial impressions of a player from their first pass, their first tackle or whatever. We should try to keep our minds open where we can to gain the most realistic and representative assessment of a player as practicably possible.

We will also see 'bandwagon bias' in scouting as in other spheres of life. Some scouts will go along with the flow of what they hear from others and adopt the image of a player that they have heard rather than objectively and independently coming to their own conclusions. If you have ever sat in a decision meeting after a trial game or whatever you will often see the bandwagon in full flow. One influential voice might say, 'The No.17 was a good player,' and a lot of other voices will fall into line and some may well not have even noticed No.17.

We see the 'bandwagon' effect go around the football world when a particular player might become flavour of the month and you hear scouts singing their praises when you know they have not actually seen the player themselves. There is nothing wrong with saying 'I haven't seen him so I don't know', but you will not hear that as much as you think you should.

There are other broader biases at play too. Some years ago I noticed that there were very few Asian kids in academies. For some academies this may reflect the general population in their area. My first assumption here is that broadly the ethnic mix of players in an academy should reflect the ethnic mix of the area they cover. There are some academies with major Bangladeshi or Pakistani communities on their doorsteps that have very few kids from these communities signed up. The more I looked at this, the more it did not make sense. Many of the communities I was looking at would have a lot of second- or third-generation young people who have grown up here in the UK in a football culture. Why are they not more represented in the academy system?

I went to see Kevin Coleman, then diversity manager at the FA, several years ago. I posed the question to him, and we had a good discussion. One worrying thing was that Kevin said I was the first person from an academy to raise the question with him. We discussed how some communities in London have done their own thing and bypassed the mainstream football structure. He mentioned he was aware of Turkish-heritage teams playing in their own set-up, for example.

Recently, in preparation for this book, I asked the question again via my social media channels. I received a wide range of responses. Some people just simply said 'they are not good enough'. I found that difficult to take – what, all of 'them'? Others said much the same along the lines of if 'they' are talented enough they will come through. At this end of the range of responses there did not seem to be much appreciation of how disadvantage works where groups or communities are concerned, and the role of equal access to opportunity and the key issue of role models, plus all the other elements that bring light and shade to discussions around disadvantage. Several people felt that many Asian cultures did not value participation and progress in sports as highly as education and employment in the professions. We can look at how some pupils attending schools such as Eton are progressing into the professional game, however, which undermines that argument a little.

There was then the discussion around parental support and whether in some Asian communities there was not the extent of parents prioritising getting their children to training or into clubs or whatever. However, the number of parents responding who clearly had actively encouraged and supported their children into football ran counter to that. One experienced grassroots coach in north-west England, Ray Woodhouse, said he felt that many Asian children in the communities he works in are not encouraged enough to start getting involved in football in their early years. Consequently, they might be coming to the game some years behind other groups of children. 'Many Asian children in our area don't start until much later in football as they get into it via school friends,' Ray told me. 'A couple of lads in my son's class have taken an interest recently because they're playing in school, but the reality is they're starting six years after some kids and it's difficult to make up time.'

At the other end of the range of views were those who felt there was racism involved. One parent echoed the views of a lot of people when he reflected on his own son's experiences in football. He said, 'I personally feel in most cases it's down to racism towards Asians being the prevalent reason you don't see Asian players in academies. I've heard young players comment on Asian players: if he was black/white he would get signed – even kids as young as 13 can see it for what it is.'

We know there is racism in football. Given there is racism in our society it would be extraordinary if it was not also reflected in football. We are, of course, part of the community and not separate from it. I have heard scouts trotting out the stereotypes on black or Asian players just as you would hear a few people in any pub bar also reflect such views.

Many years ago when I was managing in non-league at Willenhall Town FC in the West Midlands we had an away game at Chasetown. We won easily and, as was my habit right through my time as a manager, I went into the boardroom after the game, mainly to see my chairman and directors. Later, at a higher level, I would have the local media interviews to do, but after the media and the directors I would then be free to go into the players' lounges to see my guests and the players.

Anyway, on this occasion, one of the opposition directors said to me, 'Well, you were much too strong and quick for us today. Mind you, see, we don't have any of them playing for us.' It took me a good few seconds to realise who he was talking about. About half our team were black, although I had never thought about my squad in those terms.

I said, 'We've never met before, have we?'

'No, I don't think so,' said the director, quaffing his whisky.

'I hope we never meet again,' I said and walked away.

It was not just in the boardrooms that I encountered racism. The worst two grounds for racism in my experience were both in East Anglia, as I recall – Wisbech and King's Lynn. In both cases opposing fans were openly racist in their chanting and calling. This is 30 years ago, and I trust this would not happen now. But it happened then.

There have been some other well-publicised cases of racism in football. In 2018 Tony Henry, then director of player recruitment at West Ham United, was suspended following a *Daily Mail* report that he had allegedly told agents that the club did not want to sign any more African players as they 'cause mayhem' when they do not play.

In July 2018 Henry was banned from football for 12 months by the FA. And in August 2018 Manchester City started an investigation after one of their scouts allegedly referred to players as 'BBQs – big, black and quick'.

The lack of diversity in the women's game has been raised too. The website 'Her Football Hub' recently reported on how neither Arsenal nor Everton had a single black player in their squads in the Women's Super League.

Another parent – an experienced, qualified coach whose son is now playing at a good standard – was quite clear about causes but also pointed the way forward in terms of fact-finding:

> Quite simply put, Asian players are not given the same opportunity or judged with the same yardstick as other players – this is quite simply down to coaches/scouts being scared to break the mould and, in some cases I have heard, unfortunately, pure racism. I don't work in football, but in all industries I think you need to analyse the data and then make judgements from there. People in football love to quote how things are getting better; I don't think this is the case. The barrier to getting into an academy is as hard as ever for Asian footballers. I would strongly urge, if possible, to look at the data to see how many Asian footballers have been called into a club for a trial – forget for now how many are signed. The EDI statistics clubs use are misleading as they dilute this data with non-footballing roles. And it doesn't look at individual clubs or geographical areas.

The problem here is, as far as I know, clubs are not often sharing this sort of data in terms of the demographics of players invited in for trial. I would bet some academies do not even keep that data themselves.

It can be difficult to get a complete picture of this very important issue, which is a challenge not only to the game itself but to scouts who are such a crucial part of the selection process, and in a sense one of the gatekeepers to the professional game. Niaz Shazad is a finance professional at a Premier League club. He recently wrote an article – 'Asians in Football' – which brings together the facts, the current situation and the arguments on this key issue. I feel it is such an important contribution that I have, with Niaz's permission, reproduced the article in Appendix 2. The article also looks ahead to what needs to be done. I would urge you all to read it.

The answer as to why there are not more Asian players in our academies is likely to be a multifaceted one, in my view. There are some cultural barriers that some Asian youngsters would have to overcome. There is racism and there are stereotypical views of the shortcomings of Asian players affecting some scouts, and therefore some opportunities and pathways. There are consequently few role models, and we know how important it is for youngsters to see 'people like me' where they aspire to be.

From my experience, when I was out doing grassroots scouting, I just did not see that many Asian players out there on the parks in the areas I was covering.

To be fair, these were areas where there were probably not substantial Asian communities. Nevertheless, I think we need to look beyond the academies as a starting point and look at the engagement rates of Asian children in organised football.

I do remember when there were few black players in our professional teams and in our centres of excellence and training centres. In time that has changed and there is much more of a fair proportionate representation of black players in our game. It has not yet perhaps worked through to the numbers of coaches and managers, but I do think it is getting there, albeit too slowly. There are initiatives from the FA and others increasing the engagement of black and ethnic minorities in the game and I have been involved in a couple of those. Progress seems painstakingly slow.

As scouts we need to keep open minds, as I have said, with reference to many different aspects of our work. We need to guard against stereotypes making up our minds for us on players in advance, along with the other biases I have outlined. If we fail to do so we may be missing talent. That is our job – to find talent. We need to unearth it wherever it may be. Sometimes we may have to dig deep and sometimes we may even have to help even up the landscape so as not to miss that talent. We all have our parts to play.

Follow the QR link for a video from me on racism in football:

Chapter Thirteen

Being a Scout

THERE ARE many routes into scouting. My own pathway started when I had to do my own scouting when I started as a manager in non-league football. There just simply was not the staff structure that you would expect at bigger clubs or even better non-league clubs these days. I did eventually get some help in local football and in non-league football on a wider basis as I gradually built my network, but it was mainly me. However, for me, going out and watching games, assessing players and learning about them was one of the best parts of the job of being a manager.

At Willenhall Town – my first manager role – we would train two nights a week, perhaps play a midweek game and then play again on Saturdays. This is a very normal non-league routine for part-time clubs. Consequently, this meant I had one night effectively to go out to watch other teams. As mentioned earlier, I was advised by Graham Allner, then manager at Kidderminster Harriers, to switch a training night from a Tuesday to a Monday as there would be more games to watch on a Tuesday. He advised that you scout for the future. By this, he meant that as a manager you are out looking at players who may at some time in the future be what you want.

I took this advice both in terms of organising the week but also in terms of getting out and watching as many players as possible at all the various levels of non-league. I really enjoyed trying to work out whether players would fit into the sort of team I was building but, of course, this will always be within the restrictions of the budget and level of the club you are at. I loved watching the matches and gradually got to know people in the game. Those many midweek night-time fixtures in and around the West Midlands hold a lot of happy memories for me.

I recall one of the first games I went to watch was at Racing Club Warwick, and I was much taken by a flying left-winger who I learned was called Adie Fitzhugh. He was quick, had a great left foot and used the ball well. It would be a couple of months later when I realised I needed a left-sided player in the 3-5-2 formation I was then using at Willenhall Town. I recalled Adie and managed to find a way to get hold of his phone number and gave him a ring. He went on to play for me at Willenhall Town and at Atherstone United, then even later at Evesham United as well. He was a great player to have in your squad, with great touch and ability on the ball, but also a good lad to work with. I seem to recall him playing in that very first game as a winger, but he would always tell me afterwards that he was more of a left-back and it was there that I most used him in the three clubs that he played at for me.

By the time I got to Cheltenham Town as a manager, I had some people I could call upon to do some scouting. I recall that Martin McNulty would cover local football for me as we were keen to identify the best of any talent playing in the local leagues who might work for us. I also had the great fortune of John Rock, who was working for Martin O'Neill at Leicester City and became a good friend. He would help me identify players when he could fit it in between his work for Leicester. However, I still very much felt I needed to rely on my own eye and my own judgement.

We were looking for a centre-back at one point, having sold Steve Jones to Swansea, and I was asked by the FA to select and manage the FA XI for a regional game against the Combined Services team. In this role you got to pick the best players in non-league football in your region and it would all go towards helping the manager of the England C team, who was then Tony Jennings, who would be looking to bring together the England C squad. This allowed me to identify some players from other rival clubs that I liked and to see what it would be like to work with them – an unusual form of scouting, I guess!

So I was able to pair up Chris Banks, the Cheltenham Town centre-back and captain, with Mark Freeman, who was then at Gloucester City. They played well together, and I knew that if I had the chance this could be an effective centre-back pairing. It was some time later that I managed to buy Mark Freeman – known as 'Boka' – by coincidence a former Willenhall Town lad (although before my time) and get him into the Cheltenham Town team, where he played with distinction for some years. A good centre-back, a real warrior and someone that you could trust absolutely.

So my grounding in scouting started as a coach and manager, particularly in my non-league days when it was part of the job. I did a little scouting for Dario Gradi at Crewe Alexandra but it was really when I was at Portsmouth much later as a coach in one of the pre-academy development centres that I was also required to go out to scout players for these ages and older. This was an important part of the process of me learning how the centres of excellence, as they were then called, worked for the pro clubs, and it was a good grounding in grassroots scouting. I have always had a soft spot for Portsmouth and still believe that Fratton Park is one of the best places to watch football when it is full and rocking, as they are very devoted and vociferous fans.

Other scouts have different routes into the game. Staying with the Portsmouth theme, Conner Agar, one of the best young scouts around, who would later work for Bournemouth and Manchester City, started with Portsmouth at a young age. Conner told me:

> I began working voluntarily for Portsmouth helping in a matchday coordinator role when I was 17. This enabled me to be around the training ground environment. The role was a 'jack of all trades' role ranging from standing and allowing players and parents into the ground for hours on end or picking up any rubbish left in the changing rooms, to working with goalkeeper coaches and the analyst Marc Rochan, who now has a World Cup runners-up medal with Croatia.

Portsmouth allowed me to do the very first FA Talent ID certificate and I went and did some scouting when I could. Eventually, that led to creating a good relationship with the head of academy recruitment at AFC Bournemouth and I began my first paid role with them and had an enjoyable and successful seven seasons there.

Neil Sillett is now a scout for the Scotland national team and has had senior roles previously as a global scout with Aston Villa, technical director at Puerto Rico FC, and a technical scout for the Costa Rica national team. He has had many other roles, including scouting for Stoke City, Newcastle United, Brighton & Hove Albion and was also head of academy recruitment at Portsmouth FC at one stage. Neil's route into scouting was a bit different because his dad, John Sillett, was the manager at Coventry City and indeed won the FA Cup with them. Neil, or 'Sills' as he is known, told me:

I started working with my father at Coventry City in 1986 when he was appointed first team head coach/manager. I had a main role of assistant physio while gaining my medical qualifications. I also took my early coaching badges. We had a very small staff, five altogether, which meant scouting duties were shared amongst us. This meant seeing opposition and target players from the age of 23 with advice mentoring and learning from my old fella and the other staff with huge experience like Mick Coop, Terry Paine, Mick Kearns, who between them played over 2,000 games, and also head scout Ian McFarland, so it was an excellent learning ground for me. Some of the tips I still use now as, although the game has evolved, the traits of top players haven't changed.

In grassroots scouting, you will often find that people have run successful local teams in junior football or perhaps district teams and will then find their way into scouting because they already have the network that the academies know is essential to being a good scout. They may become an attractive proposition for a local academy. In fact, it was when I was managing one of my younger son's grassroots teams in a local tournament that Portsmouth came and scouted him. In a discussion with Steve Martin, who I think was then head of academy recruitment at Portsmouth, he said as well as signing my son he wanted to recruit me as a coach and scout. So I guess I came back into the game through this local experience route too.

You do have a whole generation of younger scouts now, often with sports science backgrounds, who are finding their way into the game. They may have their own roots too, but perhaps would not yet have had the opportunity to develop the years of experience of the game as a coach or manager. They will, however, have the familiarity with the data that is a growing part of the requirement of modern scouts.

Whatever your route into scouting, I think there are some things that form the basis of becoming a good scout. From one vantage point or another, perhaps as a player, coach or manager in the professional game or local football, you need to know the game. This is key and obvious. It means understanding how the game really works, who is the player that is having an influence on a game and what it is about that player that gives them this influence. You must therefore be able to understand the game and understand what contribution the various players are making to that game. You then need to build up your local knowledge of teams and players and begin to create that network. You need therefore to be approachable and someone who is ready to be a sounding board and a contact point for others. This does not suit everybody; however, as we have seen, the network is essential, so you must be open to making the sort of connections that make that network possible.

Through one means or another, you are going to have to convey your impressions of a player. This may mean you need to be able to write reports that express that opinion. The days that we characterised as 'back of a fag packet' have long gone, as we discussed earlier. All clubs will require you to communicate your impressions of a player in some guise or another. If it is not through written reports then it may well be through access to an app that enables you to put information in simply and quickly, and perhaps score a player on key performance indicators. This type of app is becoming more widespread and will continue to be so in the future. However, the point here is that just understanding who the good player is, who has potential and who does not is only the first part of the role of being a scout. You will need to demonstrate that you can communicate your opinions.

The aspiring scout should look at the qualifications that are available in the industry. The main formal network structure of qualifications is, of course, those from the FA. The FA Level 1 in Talent Identification course is free and online. It is the starting point for any scout in this country. It is harder to get on to the Level Two courses as the demand now far outstrips supply. There are other organisations that offer qualifications, such as the PFSA (Professional

Football Scouts Association) and IPSO (International Professional Scouting Organisation). Their websites will tell you more about their offering, and several scouts do go down these routes with some success. I have only gone through the FA route and have no direct personal knowledge of these independent or private organisations.

Gaining some qualification, however, would indicate to the prospective employer that you really are interested in looking professionally at being a scout and are taking steps to expand your knowledge and network. It would be difficult to imagine why someone who is really interested in being a scout has not taken the FA Level 1 in Talent Identification course, for example.

So beyond that, to get started as a scout I think it is a question of getting out and watching games and to start to compile a portfolio of reports. To some extent this will depend on the type of scouting that you want to do. If it is opposition scouting, for example, then obviously you would be compiling opposition scouting reports. Generally, what you are trying to demonstrate is that you can assess a player professionally and express that assessment effectively. The criteria and the player assessment information earlier in this book will, I hope, be a good starting place. So you might go to local non-league u18 games, for example, and report on a particular player that takes your eye, then find out some more about their background if you can, as this will be an impressive addition to the basic picture of the game that you convey. You need to be able to show by these reports that you understand the game.

If your interest is grassroots scouting, then to some extent this is a little bit more difficult. You would need to know who the players are, the teams and the level of games. Of course, without being a scout this can be a bit tricky from a safeguarding point of view. However, if you know someone who is playing local football and is happy for you to go along to the game that their son is playing in and do a report, then this is a good way in. You might get to know the coaches of a couple of local teams and explain to them what you are trying to do, and again this may be your foot in the door. I think it is important to be upfront when undertaking this sort of work, as a stranger standing on the touchline of a kids' game and taking notes might raise concerns.

In this way you can compile a portfolio of reports showing what you can do. You might then decide that you are going to approach a local academy and offer your services, or you may even apply straight for a part-time role that is advertised. Depending on your background it is likely that an academy would want to see some experience and, of course, you are then in the usual 'Catch 22' that to get a job you need to show experience and to show experience you need to get a job! However, several smaller academies do take on scouts in volunteer roles. I have some misgivings about this because in a sense it does undermine the professionalism of the role and is perhaps an indicator of how scouts are undervalued in the game. Having said that, a lot of people get into the game as a scout by volunteering as a starting position. Conner Agar earlier explained how he started voluntarily, and he has gone on to have a very good career in scouting.

You could also analyse some games or players via video. There is now a whole body of games available via YouTube and other platforms, and these give you the raw material for you to show what you can do. There are, of course, many games on TV, which can also be a very useful source of material for your scouting reports. Given the growing importance and significance of video scouting, this is a relevant tool you have in your bag.

Through all this it is important to remember that your reports are your product as a scout. Consequently, you need to make sure they are professional and well-presented. I cannot exaggerate how important this is.

So what is scouting like as a job? The starter positions in many academies may be on a voluntary basis with the smaller academies, or at the best would probably be part-time contracts. Some clubs pay on a per-game basis. It is quite common for a scout to be paid something like £50 per game for going to watch and compiling a report. Part-time contracts would usually set out a nominal number of hours per week and, through this process, it should be clear exactly what is expected of you in terms of how many games you are required to cover and what reports you need to do. This clarity is essential. Part-time roles may pay from £200 per month upwards, depending on hours.

For many people the objective would be to progress to a full-time scouting role. In general terms, I have advised many young scouts in the past that to leap to full-time you first need to be able to offer more than just scouting and, secondly, you need to be aware of the pros and cons. You need to be able to show that you have some other competencies that you can bring to bear. These may include being familiar with data and being able to manipulate it. It may be that you can show you know how to clip video reports to compile presentations on players. It may simply be that you have experience in managing people so you can show that you know how to coordinate a team and build and motivate it. There are a lot of people around who are desperate to get into full-time scouting, and if you can show an extra competence it may just lift you above the rest of the field.

Of course, for some, it may be that their experience in the game as a professional player is seen by many academies as an advantage. It is important, as I have said, to be able to demonstrate that you know the game. However, as we have seen with managers across the world, it is not essential to have been a top-class player to become a top-class manager. I think that Jose Mourinho or Arsène Wenger would be the obvious examples that spring to mind. The same is true of scouts. Some of the best scouts I have met have not had illustrious professional playing careers, because other than an understanding of the game, the skill set is different from a coach to a scout or from a player to a scout. It is connected but different.

It is also important to be aware of the pros and cons of going full-time in football in a general sense before you take that leap. This applies not only to becoming a scout on a full-time basis but also, I think, a coach or manager. When I was managing part-time I found it very difficult to juggle all the demands of a full-time ordinary job and a part-time manager role.

However, there is a security in that. You do not have all your eggs in one basket.

It must be said, though, that while you will meet many great people in football, there are not many who are good at managing other people. This is, of course, not restricted to football, but you have what is known as the 'Peter Principle', whereby people will rise up the corporate ladder to the point where they become inefficient. You can look at teaching and see many very good teachers who go on to become very mediocre head teachers. This is certainly the case in football as well. You will find people who are very good scouts, for example, who do not have a clue about how to manage people and perhaps have never really done that in any other industry. Football is a strange world. It is a small world and there are a lot of great people in it. But it is a massively insecure world.

It is sad to say that certainly in British football there is a culture that includes a strand of arrogance. It seems to suggest that because we are involved in football, possibly at a high level, we can treat people however we like. There is always going to be a queue of people down the road outside the training ground desperate to get in. This contributes to instances of very inefficient and clumsy management. I have said before that scouting is the last part of football to become professionalised. Nowhere is this more apparent than when you look at the standards of staff management.

I have been very fortunate overall. There are lots of good managers out there and gradually the game is getting its act in order and extending its professionalism to include modern standards and practice of staff management. However, I do think if you want to get into scouting you need to be aware that you may well be working for people in senior positions who have never had any management training at all. I am not suggesting that you do not take that step if it is in front of you and if it is your ambition. However, I strongly suggest that you think very carefully and find out all you can about the people who you are going to be working for. I suppose it is like being a scout, in terms of doing your due diligence. It is common sense to do your due diligence on prospective managers.

I have stood on the touchline with many friends who are in scouting or have sat talking over a coffee and heard horror stories about the way they have been treated. Football at all levels can be very cut-throat and unfair. Unfortunately, there do seem to be some people in positions of authority who feel, based on the way they act at times, that normal employment law and normal standards of treatment of staff do not apply to them, simply because they are in football. Again I stress that this is not universal, but it is prevalent enough that you should be aware that it is out there, so take care.

So what practical resources do you need to be a scout? In general terms, you will need transport. I know of a few good scouts such as Dave Allan of Manchester United who do not drive and have managed to get to all sorts of grounds to watch games using public transport. To some extent it will depend on where you are working and what the public transport network is like in the areas that you will need to cover.

Generally though, clubs will require you to have your own transport so you can get around to whatever games you are required to cover. This is perhaps slightly less important if you are doing grassroots scouting as it may be more localised. If you are in an urban area you may well be able to get by without a car. Broadly though, it is expected that you have your own transport. You will hopefully be paid mileage for the cost that you incur, but I would not take that for granted!

When you get to a game, you are going to need to find a way to record your notes to help you produce your report. For some this will be the trusty notebook, and I have a collection of many of these tracking back over several years. In fact, I have them in various sizes – from a pocket-sized A6 book for touchline work to a fuller A5 or even A4 for when I know I will be sitting in a stand. You will find your own way of recording notes and information. We do find in the modern world that many scouts are happy recording the information on their phones, and this is probably even more common than the old-fashioned notebooks now. It has the advantage that you can easily store your notes and even print them off if you want.

Lastly, increasingly clubs are using apps on which you can record the information that is required on a player or a team. Again this will vary according to what sort of scouting you are doing. If you are doing first-team scouting in a live situation and are really doing an in-depth report on an individual player, then you might need to be able to track their movement and record some basic performance data, as I have covered earlier. This may be a notebook or one of the customised apps that are now available to help you do that.

One of the main considerations of whichever method you use, and depending on where you are going to be doing your scouting, will be what happens when it is pouring down with rain. One thing I can guarantee in this country is that if you are a scout you will be getting soaking wet more regularly than you probably would wish! So, it is fine using a notebook but when it is raining that is difficult, and even using a phone can be awkward sometimes in heavy rain.

I remember going to a game at Portsmouth down at the university ground on the 4G, where Portsmouth u18s were playing Oxford United u18s. I was there with my mate Dave Allan of Manchester United. It absolutely threw it down for the entire time. It was unrelenting, like a monsoon. I quite soon gave up on my notebook as there was too much rain to make notes. I then started making notes on my phone but eventually had to give that up as it was getting too wet. I was finally reduced to just standing there with the rain hammering down, feeling that I was getting soaking wet and hoping my memory would allow me to make my report afterwards. I can remember turning to Dave and saying, 'What are we doing here?' Oh, the joys of scouting!

So, given our climate, you will need to kit yourself out with a properly waterproof coat, trousers and shoes, and maybe you will be able to use an umbrella, although I have always found that very cumbersome. One of the best tips I was given when I started scouting with Chelsea was from the great scout Ray Rembridge, who brought in Reece James and many others to the club. He opened the boot of his car to show me a bag full of different sorts of kit. He had clothes for just about every season. If it is really hot you might need to change into shorts or a T-shirt. If it is cold you are going to need extra layers. You may need an umbrella or a hat, gloves, snood, scarf or anything else you can think of. The point is that Ray had it all in the boot of his car because in our climate, as we know, we can experience all seasons within the course of one afternoon. I have done the same ever since. This is an advantage of having a car, of course.

Clubs may provide your kit. The big academies would normally issue at least a coat to scouts. As discussed in the section on grassroots scouting, many clubs will want you to be identified as being from them as it helps in safeguarding, and in terms of brand recognition. However, if you are doing academy scouting it is not normal practice to wear something that identifies the club that you work for.

It is a funny thing but, as you gain more experience, you can spot scouts a mile away. As I write this I recall I was at a game at Worthing recently, watching the first team, and I knew the two guys sitting behind me were scouts, although I did not recognise them. Firstly, I knew because one of them had managed to get the team sheet from somewhere and most fans would not bother, and, secondly, they looked like the conventional scout. This means they were middle-aged or older white men and wore thick winter coats – the same description would apply to me of course! The diversity of scouts is changing and can only be a good thing, but it is slow progress.

So life as a scout if you are covering grassroots football means you will be out and about in your area learning about your patch, building your network, as we have covered in Chapter Six. You will be watching as many games as you can, perhaps at the target age groups you have been set. This means you are out on Saturday and Sunday mornings and maybe Sunday afternoons for the most part. You might be visiting other soccer schools or clubs when they are training during the week. You will be constantly on the phone and checking social media, gathering information, gathering intelligence and building that network.

If you are doing academy scouting, opposition scouting or first-team scouting, you will spend a lot of time on the road, although for opposition and first-team scouting at the senior levels it means you will spend a lot of time in front of a video screen! But travelling around, getting to games through all sorts of weather where your trusty 'sat nav' will be your best friend, is very much part of the traditional role. Expect hours on the road. Over the years I have discovered all the best places to get a bacon sandwich on a Sunday morning when visiting certain academy training grounds. You will find your way around.

You will also be spending a lot of time on your laptop or PC doing reports. This does vary from one role to another but generally it is going to be the case, and if you are not happy doing those reports then you need to think carefully about this. For pretty much all types of scouting you will be expected to be on the internet checking the key websites and social media feeds to be gathering information and gossip. This is part of the role of being a scout, as I have emphasised. It is not just about watching a game and deciding whether you like a player or not, it is about finding out everything that you can about that player. It is about rechecking and going back and watching that player again wherever you can.

It will also mean working as a team with other colleagues, cross-checking players and sharing information. It will certainly mean you doing your due diligence and becoming familiar with all the information that can be gleaned from the internet and social media these days. You are going to spend a lot of time on WhatsApp or similar, communicating with your club and the other scouts. This is all part of the role of the scout, and if it is not something that you feel you can do or feel comfortable with then I suggest you think twice.

It can be a lonely job as you are out on your own for the most part. If you are working for a club that is some distance away, then you will not have the contact and connection that is possible for a local club. In these circumstances, scouts can really feel isolated and that they are a long distance from their club in all manner of ways. Of course, good academies will work to minimise these effects by having good communication lines and good personal development programmes, getting the scouts into the training ground, watching first-team games and feeling part of the club whenever that is possible and practical.

I would also stress again that as a scout you are part of a team and your opinion is often one of many that might be gathered on a particular player. Throughout his book, when I have been mentioning my opinions on players I was asked to report on, it would invariably be the case that my voice was just one of a number raised on that player. Some scouts find this difficult to deal with. I must say it has never bothered me, as I can see scouting has been moving to a team game.

So there is good and bad to being a scout. You are out in all weathers. You are often unsung and unappreciated. You are usually poorly paid and often badly managed. There is perhaps no real recognition or appreciation of your role in general within the game. However, if you love football then the excitement of discovering a new talent is a major attraction. I have always found it an exciting moment as you are awaiting the start of any game, because you never know what you will find. Players can turn up in the strangest of places, and even assessing a player and deciding they are not for you is a very interesting process. I have always found scouting to be intellectually challenging, requiring you to be always open to learning and to appreciate that you never know the full picture.

You will meet some good people. I do not want to give a negative picture of the scouting game at all because there are some great characters who you will encounter along the way. It is great, too, to play a part in helping a young player make their way into the game, and hugely satisfying when they do well. So, overall, I would say you need to be realistic about scouting and understand the reality of it, and that includes how much the game needs to improve in certain areas. Equally, though, I would not be doing it justice if I do not say it can be great fun. You will be a key part of the lovely, crazy world of football. And there is always another game ...

Follow the QR link to me speaking about how to become a scout:

Chapter Fourteen

It Starts and Ends with Players

I FIRST saw Shimmy Mheuka play when he was ten years old. He was playing for Brighton's u11s and mostly played as a central defender, although he did have a short time playing up front. He was playing against Chelsea, who I was working for at the time, in a normal academy game. I knew of him because I was aware we had wanted to sign him when he was eight years old, but his family then lived in Burgess Hill near Brighton, as I recall, and the distance was just a bit too far to be practical.

He had a very good physical shape, slim and athletic. He was very composed on the ball and seemed to find it easy playing at the back with the game in front of him. He read the game well and covered the ground easily. He played the ball well and was able to bring it out of defence with some style. I was really impressed by him, and he was clearly a player that we would want to track.

Over the next few years I came across him quite often. Before long he was playing up a year and seemed to play quite often as a forward, in fact as a central attacker. The original performance as a defender stuck in my mind and I felt through that time that he looked more comfortable as a defender than he did as a striker. However, he was a good all-round player and a good athlete. Brighton persevered with him as a striker and often played him up one or two years. I reported on him many times. I watched him in all weather and in all types of games. Sometimes he was as effective as others, and I was not sure that always playing him up necessarily worked in his favour in all instances. He would often be up against stronger, more physical defenders, and although he never shied away from the physical part of the game it did not seem to my mind to always be of benefit to him. However, he continued to thrive and by the time he was a u14 regularly playing in Brighton's u15s and even u16s at times, most scouts on the circuit would say he was probably the best striker of his age group in the country.

In most clubs you have meetings of scouts where you are asked your opinions as to who should be a priority and who the club should target. At those meetings it was common – again as it is in most clubs – for scouts to be asked, 'If you could sign one player who would it be?' This is a bit of an old chestnut in that it does depend on what the club's priorities are at that moment. However, it is a reasonable question to ask. It got so that I would always say 'Shimmy'. I thought he was the best striker of his age group that I had seen anywhere. He was often a standout playing up as well, and he was scoring goals of all different types. He was ready to work and apply himself and, as he grew into his physical shape, he became a powerful and athletic forward. I did my due diligence on him and discovered that he was a good scholar, well thought of at his school and had a strong and supportive family background.

Scouting nowadays is a team effort. I was just one of many scouts who reported on Shimmy and overall their feelings and opinions were very positive. However, I guess I had been watching him for probably the longest of the scouts then doing academy scouting at the club. So I very much identified with him.

Chelsea eventually signed him from Brighton at the end of his u14 season. I understand that a lot of the big clubs were interested in him and it was a great coup for Chelsea to sign such a talent. He is a regular for England under-17s now and is progressing very well at the club. He has a great future in front of him. When he was signed the club invited me to his signing presentation. His delighted family were in attendance, of course, and his dad Malcolm, who is a real gentleman, gave me a big bear hug when he saw me and said, 'You know, we've seen you over the years come in to watch Shimmy, season in and season out, and it's great that you have finally been able to sign him.' I had not been able to speak to the family on any of those occasions; however, Malcolm added, 'You've always been very professional, but we always knew that you were there.'

That is a good learning point for scouts. You are there to watch but maybe you are being watched too.

The journey for Shimmy was a long one over several years, and I was a part of a process that involved a lot of other scouts. This is often the reality of modern scouting at a large academy. However, for all that, I did get a real sense of satisfaction that the player I had spotted in that first game and had been tracking so assiduously over the years was finally signed.

I can remember one time in particular watching Shimmy play for Brighton's u15s against Millwall on a miserable wet night at Brighton's training ground at Lancing, on the 4G pitch. It was a Midweek Floodlit Cup game. It was a dark and dismal winter evening.

This is the reality of scouting, that you will be tracking a player in all conditions. In fact, it is important to see how a player deals with different conditions, different pitches and different opponents. It is all part of the process of assessment. Unfortunately, it means you, as a scout, have to suffer those conditions too!

It is funny how scouting works. Even though I have left Chelsea now I will still get satisfaction from seeing Shimmy progress, hopefully get into top-flight football and play in the Premier League one day. I will still feel a sense of pride that I have played my little part in his progress. This is the good side of scouting – where you see the talent, you identify them, you track them and eventually, they get signed. Then you can see them fly. However, meanwhile, you are on to the next game and the next player.

The best player I have ever seen? The next one.

The last video from me for this book:

Appendix 1

PFSA Code of Conduct for Scouts

From website pfsa.org.uk:

To help advance and preserve this trust, the Professional Football Scouts Association has developed this Code of Conduct designed to serve as a guide and reference for our behaviour and also a reference for our members to act accordingly whilst carrying out their duties.

These include:

- Promote high standards of behaviour.
- Never engage in offensive, insulting or abusive language or behaviour towards fellow members and players, match officials, parents, spectators, coaches, team managers and club officials.
- Avoid bullying, intimidation and poor behaviour towards fellow members and

players, match officials, parents, spectators, coaches, team managers, and club officials.

- Never discriminate any fellow member and player, match official, parent, spectator, coach, team manager, or club official regardless of age, ethnicity, gender or race.

- Do not instruct players on what to do whilst observing them play on your scouting duties.

- A professional football scout should be honest, respectful, and truthful towards fellow members and players, match officials, parents, spectators, coaches, team managers, and club officials.

- A professional football scout should carry out their duties in compliance with the laws of the country.

- Adhere to all rules and regulations at all times and adhere to the laws of the game.

- Never interfere with the field of play.

- Ensure the parents/carers of all players under the age of 18 understand these expectations.

- Co-operate fully with fellow members and players, match officials, parents, spectators, coaches, team managers, and club officials.

Asians In Football – by Niaz Shazad

INTRO

British Football has a distinct lack of South Asian representation, be it on-field players and management, or off it through fans, administrators, and senior leadership. But why?

The PFA's Asian Inclusion Mentoring Scheme's (AIMS) most recent update showed the number of players at all levels of elite football identifying as of South Asian heritage was 134 – but broken down further, 92 of these exist within the foundation and youth development phases, 25 scholars and merely 17 at professional level.

To put that into context, the Premier League requires 25 players to be registered per club in the league. Compound that with many clubs having B teams, U21s, U19s, U17s, U14s, academies, etc. and it's not an exaggeration to state many clubs likely have more than 134 players just on their own books. If we take a mere scan at the top four domestic leagues, there are over 2,500 players registered to partake – and that's before we get into any of the age brackets beyond first teams.

For too long, throwaway remarks like, *'He's too small ...' & 'better off going and playing cricket '...'* have been the unfortunate norm in our game. Dave Bassett, former manager of Wimbledon, Sheffield United and various others and with over 1,000 games under his belt, in a BBC appearance went one further: *'... the Asian build is not that of a footballer [...] It may well be that Asian ingredients in food, or the nutrition they take, [is] not ideal for building up a physical frame' (BBC TV 1995, in Fleming 2001: 114).* But the recent comments from Crystal Palace's lead pre-academy scout are arguably even more unfortunate: *'Asian families put all their efforts into education plus their [sic] more aligned to the game of cricket ... Don't think it's pushed in their families or in their culture ... Boys following this sport are far and few in this industry.'*

Given the demographics of the constituency Palace are located within, and the fact these thoughts are still in existence in 2023 – one can only wonder how many talents have been wasted due to the pre-conceived biases.

However, despite popular belief, **Football, and not Cricket, is the number one sport for British Asians** (Burdsey 2007; Saeed & Kilvington 2011; Kilvington & Price 2013). Given the proportion of the population at large coupled with their passion for the sport, observations such as Dave Bassett's being passed down the generations, cultural beliefs and/or societal generalisations, it's led to the existence of a glaring inconsistency – South Asians being few and far between within football.

So what exactly is it that's leading to such discrepancies, what's being done about it, and what more can be done? Let's explore and to set the scene, rewind the clock some four decades to a time when black footballers were similarly few and far between within British football.

BLACK REPRESENTATION PARALLELS

Bananas being thrown and disgusting monkey noises by 'fans', occasionally at players who even represented their own clubs, were sadly the norm. Elland Road heard cries of 'Leeds are White', with terraces scattered with National Front leaflets, whilst less than 50 black players operated across the entire Football League – the Premier League through to League Two as we know it today. The decade even ended in 1979 with a bizarre testimonial – Len Cantello's West Bromwich Albion against an 'All Blacks' team of those abused and discriminated against, marshalled by Cantello's team-mate Cyrille Regis.

Fast forward a generation, and Arsenal became the first English team to field nine black players in a competitive game – a couple of years later, after attracting ironic comment on 'British-ness' from Alan Pardew, Arsène Wenger was stout in his response:

> 'It's a regressive way of thinking and I would never want to say to a player, "You are better but you do not have the right passport." When you represent the club, for me it's about value and quality. It's not about passports unless we change the rules. We do nothing wrong. I try to choose the best player and I think my pride in my career is not to have chosen someone because of his passport.'

The Black Footballers Partnership (BFP) commissioned Professor Stefan Szymanski to examine black representation in English professional football over the past few years. Its findings are as follows:

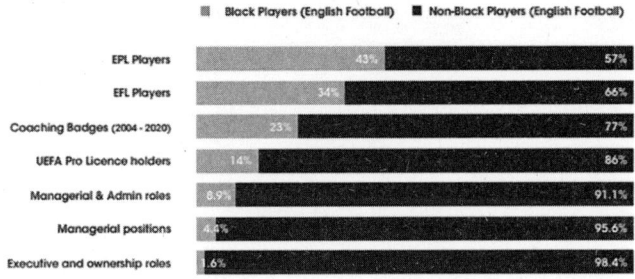

Black Football Partnership Self-reported ethnicity, England and Wales, 2021 Census

- 43% of EPL players are black.
- 1 in 3 Football League players are black.
- 1 in 7 UEFA Pro Licence holders are black.

In contrast only 4.4% occupied managerial positions and a mere 1.6% in exec and ownership. Given the shattering of the glass ceiling on the field, it seems there now exists one off it.

But how does it compare in other sports?

Within the NBA, as Figure 2 illustrates, representation of black players transitioning into coaching and management is much greater, and although still unrepresented vs. players, it's a far cry from the 4.4% and 1.6% holding relative equals in British football.

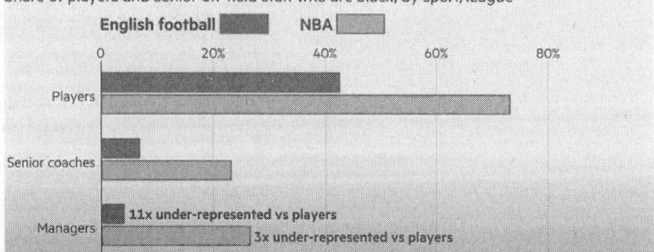

Figure 2 – Financial Times

WHAT IS BEING DONE?

The FA recognised and looked to initiate change by introducing the Football Leadership Diversity Code (FLDC), which, although welcome, has not moved the dial notably, with FA CEO Mark Bullingham acknowledging in their latest annual release '... that the game is making slower progress than hoped in diversifying its leadership, coaching staff and workforce'. Adoption of this code has been voluntary since its inception three years ago, and as the snippet opposite shows, not a single target was met at club level, indicative of the relatively relaxed approach thus far in the Premier League post 2022/23. In addition:

- 8 out of 18 clubs reported zero hires in senior leadership from diverse backgrounds.
- 9 out of 17 reported zero hires in coaching.

- Only 6 clubs reported meeting the target for team operations.

- Only 4 clubs reported meeting the target in coaching.

Code Segment	Targets		Clubs	FA/PL/EFL	Collective Football Average
SENIOR LEADERSHIP TARGETS	15%	of our new hires will be Black, Asian or of Mixed Heritage (or a target set by the club based on local demographics)	9.1%	27.3%	9.4%
	30%	of our new hires will be female	23.0%	36.4%	23.3%
TEAM OPERATIONS TARGETS	15%	of our new hires will be Black, Asian or of Mixed Heritage (or a target set by the club based on local demographics)	11.2%	20.2%	11.7%
	30%	of our new hires will be female	29.9%	47.1%	31.0%
COACHING- MEN'S CLUBS TARGETS	25%	of our new hires will be Black, Asian or of Mixed Heritage	16.0%	50.0%	16.2%
	10%	of our new senior coaching hires will be Black, Asian or of Mixed Heritage	8.9%	100.0%	9.4%
COACHING- WOMEN'S CLUBS TARGETS	50%	of our new hires will be female	41.6%	50.0%	42.1%
	15%	of our new hires will be Black, Asian or of Mixed Heritage	8.3%	16.7%	8.8%

With the need to evolve, however, there is a change in the offing – English football has agreed 'in principle' to make reporting of diversity data compulsory from the start of the 2024/25 season, so should allow for deliberation over not only ethnicities but also age, sex, gender, sexual orientation and disability data respectively.

The PFA, the FA, the EFL and the Premier League all have 'Action Plans', some of which we will touch upon through this piece, whilst Sky Sports have the dedicated services of Dev Trehan with a regular South Asian Football column – recently named as the inaugural winner of the Diversity in Media Award at the 2023 Asian Media Awards. I was unable to locate an equivalent dedicated hub on the BBC, nor find much in the public domain from either Amazon (Prime) or TNT Sports.

At club level, Manchester City enlisted Sevvy Aslam last year – the first, and to date only South Asian academy manager in English football, who spent over a decade at Port Vale to focus and enhance its drive for inclusivity.

From the introduction of specific provisions of halal meals and dedicated praying facilities, to the recent addition of Jummah Friday Prayers led by an imam, City are amongst a small batch of clubs implementing progressive change. Select examples also exist of great work at Bradford City (Football for Peace), Blackburn Rovers and Arsenal (Fan experience).

BUT DO SOUTH ASIANS WANT TO PLAY FOOTBALL?

The answer is a resounding Yes. Black representation, whilst combatting to some degree the on-field equivalence, now seems to face a challenge off it.

However, the most recent census from 2021 highlights persons self-identifying as Asian accounted for almost 6 million residents of the UK population – a 2.5x multiple of persons identifying as black.

The FA Asian Inclusion Plan: Progress Report August 2023

Ethnic minority groups: England (includes Wales)	2011	%	2021	%	Asian Population split by regional groupings
Indian communities	1,412,958	2.5	1,864,318	3.1	
Pakistani communities	1,124,511	2.0	1,587,819	2.7	South Asian
Bangladeshi communities	447,201	0.8	644,881	1.1	
Chinese communities	393,141	0.7	445,619	0.7	East Asian
Asian, Asian British or Asian Welsh: Other Asian	835,720	1.5	972,783	1.6	Other Asian/Mixed Heritage or
Mixed or Multiple ethnic groups: White and Asian	341,727	0.6	488,225	0.8	Multiple ethnic groups with Asian Heritage
Other ethnic group: Arab	230,600	0.4	331,844	0.6	Arab
Total	**4,785,858**	**8.5**	**6,335,489**	**10.6**	

Male Players (16+)			9,022,050 Known Population Size		
Ethnicity	Jul-19	Jul-20	Jul-21	Jul-22	Jul-23
White (British & Irish)	77%	80.0%	77.4%	76.0%	78.0%
Non-white (see breakdown below)	21.6%	18.5%	19.9%	21.6%	19.6%
Prefer not to say	2%	1.5%	2.7%	2.4%	2.3%
Ethnicity breakdown					
Mixed/multi-ethnic (White & Black Caribbean, White & Black African or Other multi-ethnic)	2.2%	1.8%	2.4%	2.3%	2.1%
Asian (Indian, British Indian, Pakistani, British Pakistani, Bangladeshi, British Bangladeshi, Chinese, British Chinese, Other Asian, British Asian or White & Asian)	12.9%	10.7%	10.4%	11.3%	10.0%
Black (Caribbean, British Caribbean, African, British African, Other Black or Black British)	5.7%	5.0%	6.0%	6.8%	6.3%
British Arab, Other Arab	0.3%	0.7%	0.5%	0.8%	0.8%
Other	0.5%	0.4%	0.7%	0.4%	0.4%

The data above from the FA's inclusion plan shows that despite 10% of the population translating relatively scamlessly into 10% of grassroots participation, of the circa 900,000 16+ male players who play the game – merely 17 have made their way into professional setups.

2023/24 South Asian Data Summary

- **29% increase** in South Asian representation of professional players in the 2023/24 season.
- In the 2022/23 season, there was a **12.6% increase** in the number of players at all levels of elite football identifying as of South Asian heritage, rising to **134 players from 119** in the previous 2021/22 season.
- The proportion of academies with at least one player of South Asian heritage grew to **63%** in the latest season, up from 53% in the 2021/22 season.
- Scholars of South Asian heritage represent 1.45% of the total, with their numbers showing an almost **9% increase** from the 2021-22 season.

Asian Inclusion Mentoring Scheme (AIMS) update 2023

From the PFA's data, 63% of academies in the UK were celebrated for having at least one player of South Asian heritage, whilst scholars represented 1.45% of the entire total. Given the huge disparities in the numbers exhibiting black representation in football, the representation of South Asians in footballing corridors in relative terms is near non-existent.

SO WHAT'S STOPPING THEM?

Several factors have contributed towards this state of play.

- Lack of role models – for every Hamza Choudhary, thousands falling by the wayside may have led to youngsters deciding upon alternative paths.
- Limited reach of scouting networks/ talent ID resulting in gifted individuals being overlooked.
- Systemic biases inadvertently or explicitly excluding South Asian players.
- Limited access to support (networks) and infrastructure (coaching, facilities, financial support, etc.).
- Socioeconomic factors stemming from historical challenges faced by immigrant communities.

There are of course exceptions to the norm – Yousuf Sajjad, formerly of both Chelsea and Arsenal, and someone prominent in the early stages of the careers of now established stars such as Billy Gilmour (Brighton), Ethan Ampadu (Leeds) and Ian Maatsen

(Chelsea), has moved to the Dutch second division club FC Den Bosch to get his first crack as technical director. Yousuf didn't carry an illustrious playing/coaching career to fall back on. But his vision coupled with an unwavering dream, which in his early days saw him use his modest retail wages to go and scout at football matches, unbeknown to his parents, and saw him refine a skill set which no doubt a top tier club will look at in the near future. Per above, the socioeconomic factors, limited network and lack of role models didn't stop him, but not everyone has a drive like Yousuf's.

Yasir Sufi, another behind the scenes doing great things at Blackburn Rovers, recently referenced how for Muslim South Asian parents/families, priorities generally tend to go as follows – Faith, Family, Food, Football.

> 'Given the prioritisation of Islamic education in the evenings (Mon-Fri) seen as a must for most 4-11 year olds, the inevitable clash with training times for the majority of grassroots clubs and academies means children of South Asian Muslim heritage, will have a lot less contact hours with a football. Therefore their talent has to be even greater to be noticed.'

It's important to note in areas such as Blackburn, Burnley and Bradford, amongst others, this is a very characteristic scenario given the demography.

Add to that deprivation – 47% of children living in Pakistani households, and 41% of children living in Bangladeshi households were living in low income. This was 30 and 24 percentage points higher, respectively, than children living in white British households and 27 and 21 percentage points higher than the national average.

In 2021, Professor Imran Awan and Dr Irene Zempi conducted interviews with 40 male and female players at grassroots football organisations who all identified as British Muslims, aged between 19 and 45.

https://bcuassets.blob.core.windows.net/docs/awan-and-zempi-report-11-feb-2021- 132593302460533798.pdf

The researchers found participants reporting experiences of hate crime from members of the public, as well as from players of opposing teams and management.

Kick It Out received a record 1,007 reports of discriminatory behaviour in the 2022/23 season from Pro Game all the way down to Grassroots – a marked 65.1% increase on the previous season. Just under half of these were directly race related (49.3%).

And the key point to note: these are only those reported. As Professor Awan states in his report:

66
We found the scope of this problem is being hidden because victims are afraid to speak out.   99
Imran Awan, Professor of Criminology

WHAT ARE THE BENEFITS OF INCLUSION OF SOUTH ASIANS?

Broadly, diversity in football is not just about representation or inclusion, it is a catalyst for improved performance and success. It is a powerful asset that significantly enhances performance in the realm of football. Clubs that embrace diversity harness the collective strengths of players and staff alike leading to enhanced team dynamics, creativity, communication, strategic thinking and what everyone's after, results. By recognising and leveraging the power of diversity, teams can achieve greater success on and off the field.

PERFORMANCE BENEFITS

- Ron Atkinson, pre his 2004 faux pax, was lauded for bringing together the affectionately termed 'three degrees' – Laurie Cunningham, Brendon Batson and Cyrille Regis to his West Brom team in 1978/79, and led the club to a third-place top-tier finish – never achieved by WBA before or since.

- 87% of France's 2018 World Cup-winning team was made up of either direct or indirect immigrants, i.e. whose parents or other generation of forefather immigrated.

- Manchester City's all-conquering squad of 22/23 was made up of 12 different nationalities and a variety of cultural backgrounds.

COMMERCIAL BENEFITS

- Borussia Dortmund's approach of recruiting American Christian Pulisic not only bolstered the team's performance but also expanded its presence in the United States. Known affectionately as 'Captain America', Pulisic's popularity helped Dortmund gain a larger following in the American market, resulting in increased revenues and brand recognition.

- Tottenham Hotspur, with their signing of Son Heung-min, helped propel their global appeal significantly – around 12 million South Koreans, almost a quarter of the entire population, are estimated to be Spurs fans. Their friendly match against a K-League team last summer was the most streamed sporting event in the nation's history, with two million viewers tuning in. South Korea is now the club's second-largest e-commerce market, making twice as many purchases as the USA.

- Juventus and Manchester United, similarly, by signing players such as South Korean international Park Ji-sung and Japanese star player Hidetoshi Nakata, expanded their reach into the lucrative Asian market. Their presence in the squad helped them gain a larger fan base in Asia, rubber-stamping their share of the market leading to increased commercial opportunities and marketing revenues in the region.

There are six million persons identifying as Asians in the UK – a huge segment of the market which is waiting to be tapped into – increased match attendances, memberships, sponsorships, food and beverage sales, etc. could all be tailored for a personalised matchday experience.

SOCIETAL BENEFITS

- Liverpool fans embraced Mohamed Salah as one of their own, with his own chant referencing his Muslim beliefs. Interestingly, a study produced by Stanford University in the USA found that since Salah signed for

Liverpool there has been an 18.9% drop in the number of hate crimes in the Merseyside area, and the number of anti-Muslim tweets posted by the club's supporters had halved.

- Didier Drogba being given the platform to showcase his abilities meant he earned legendary status back home in Ivory Coast – so much so that upon qualification for the 2006 World Cup, Drogba made a plea for peace, asking combatants to lay down their arms. His message carried such weight, it contributed to a ceasefire in the country's civil war.

- Mesut Özil, German footballer of Turkish descent, advocated regularly for integration and diversity. His success in the German national team helped promote the idea of multiculturalism in Germany.

Outside of football and from an academic angle, various studies have been undertaken showing the benefits of diverse teams in terms of productivity, innovation, and problem-solving abilities:

- McKinsey & Company Report (2015): McKinsey conducted a comprehensive study examining the relationship between diversity and financial performance. They found that companies in the top quartile for ethnic and racial diversity in management were **35%** more likely to have financial returns above their respective national industry medians. In the UK, greater gender diversity on the senior-executive team corresponded to the highest performance uplift: for every 10% increment in gender diversity, **EBIT rose by 3.5 percent.**

https://www.mckinsey.com/capabilities/people-and-organizational-performance/our-insights/why-diversity-matters

- Harvard Business Review (2016): A study published in HBR revealed that cognitively diverse teams solve problems faster than teams of cognitively similar individuals. The research highlighted that diversity in perspectives and backgrounds **fosters creativity and better decision-making.**

https://hbr.org/2017/03/teams-solve-problems-faster-when-theyre-more- cognitively-diverse

- Boston Consulting Group (BCG) Study (2017): BCG conducted a study examining diversity and innovation. They found that companies with more diverse management teams have **19% higher innovation revenues.** *https://www.bcg.com/publications/2018/how-diverse-leadership-teams-boost- innovation*

These are merely a few pertinent examples to evidence the vast array of positives which exist for clubs to take advantage of. Both from a sporting and non-sporting context therefore, the continued exclusion of South Asians is baffling.

WHAT CAN BE DONE?

Football has the power to bring people together like no other social connection. Therefore, the relevance of representation and diversity within football has never been greater. From Brazil to Bangladesh, Peru to Pakistan, the game is loved with equal vigour and enthusiasm. Football can help challenge stereotypes, define societal make-ups and break down barriers.

The premise of this article isn't to preach, but to shine a light upon an anomaly too often overlooked; spoken of but ignored when it comes to tangible changes. The following are a checklist of sorts – acknowledge, discuss, share or implement, the decision lies with you:

- Increased Representation: Encouraging more South Asian representation in coaching staff, administrative roles, and leadership positions within football clubs can help create a more inclusive environment, and remove that echo chamber.

- Targeted Outreach and Development Programmes: Initiatives aimed at identifying and nurturing talent within South Asian communities, coupled with mentorship programmes and scholarships, can provide the necessary support and opportunities.

- Education and Awareness: Raising awareness about the importance of diversity and inclusion in football and dispelling stereotypes through education and outreach programmes can help change perceptions and biases. Discuss Ramadhan and Eid, and Hanukkah and Diwali and Easter and tap into the knowledge and experience of institutions such as Sporting Equals.

- Collaboration and Support: Collaboration between football clubs, grassroots organisations, educational institutions, and community leaders is crucial to address systemic barriers and provide holistic support to aspiring South Asian players. Nujum Sports are involved cross-sport; Anwar Uddin is the FA's Diversity and Inclusion Manager, whilst Dev Trehan does wonderful work at Sky Sports via his South Asians in Football feed to name but a few.

CONCLUDING THOUGHTS

Football was born in my own backyard in Sheffield, before being shared and loved across the globe. I fell in love with the game watching (and often spending hours on Ceefax) Les Ferdinand, David Ginola and Nobby Solano. Though, as someone carrying South Asian roots and hugely passionate about the game, I'm longing for the day we see a list which reads names like Khan, Ahmed, Singh and Patel. Names of people who look like me. Talk like me. Walk like me. Because they exist. But that will only happen when the gatekeepers change the locks.

We must strive for more inclusive recruitment practices, positive role-modelling of personnel, educate and eliminate pre-conceived biases, collaborate with community organisations, and keep battling to do far more.

My father, like many first- and second-generation immigrants who crossed lands to call the UK home, working multiple manual labour jobs to set up base for himself and provide for and help settle his extended family – the priority was understandably education, and not wanting for his children what he had to endure himself.

But the United Kingdom he first called home was a lot different to the one we occupy now. As someone in a privileged position within football of South Asian heritage, and experiencing first-hand the many ups and downs only football can provide, it's disappointing therefore in some form we're still residing in the UK my father first came to and haven't progressed.

Together, let's change that. It's high time South Asians were represented proportionally in the beautiful game.

Niaz is a finance professional at a Premier League club. He oversees both men's operations and women's football holistically. He is also a candidate on the PFA's Global Sporting Directorship, as well as studying for his coaching badges with a goal of becoming a sporting director.

Acknowledgements

I HAVE been very fortunate to have a lot of people help me along the pathway that this book has taken.

In the beginning, when I was putting the book together, Xabi de Beristain Humphreys from Division X agency put me in touch with Dan Freedman. Dan is the author of the excellent Jamie Johnson series of books, among others. Dan discussed my idea with me and gave me some practical advice and encouragement. He suggested I try Pitch Publishing as a possible publisher. I got in touch with them and here we are! Jane Camillin of Pitch Publishing has been great to work with and I appreciate their faith in me and this project. I would also like to thank Ivan Butler for his excellent work editing the book. I guess that little sequence is a good example of developing and using your network, which is a key part of being a scout!

I have had support and interview time with Neil Sillett, Martin Bewell and Conner Agar. I have had advice in promoting the book from Sean Conlon of the excellent 'We Make Footballers' network, Danny Infield of Red 6 agency and particularly CJ Brough, my social media guru.

I must thank Niaz Shazad for his excellent article on 'Asians in Football' and for allowing me to reproduce it in this book. I would also like to thank Yousuf Sajjad, Technical Director at Den Bosch FC, for our conversations on the issue too.

I have had the great fortune to work alongside some excellent scouts, and much of the good stuff in this book is what I have learned from them. However, there are too many to name, but they know who they are! I must say, though, that the opinions expressed here are mine alone and I am not representing anyone else in putting them forward.

Finally, and most importantly, I must thank my wife, Julie, for her unwavering support and encouragement, particularly when this book and all that went along with it seemed to be getting me into all sorts of trouble. She has not only been directly involved in proofreading and editing the initial draft, but she has also walked every step of the way with me.

It's a team game.